TOWARD SPIRITUAL SECURITY

TOWARD
SPIRITUAL
SECURITY

by

WESNER FALLAW

Philadelphia
THE WESTMINSTER PRESS

Library of Congress Catalogue Card Number: 52–7117

PRINTED IN THE UNITED STATES OF AMERICA

To My Father
REV. HENRY MELTON FALLAW
(1873–1948)
who would have valued this work, and
To My Son
THOMAS LEE FALLAW
(1945–   )
who has contributed to certain of these pages

CONTENTS

PREFACE

We are acutely aware that personal, national, and world affairs are quick-paced and so dangerous as to make human existence tenuous. Any sensitive person is forced to recognize that all around him are people whose confusion and troubles range from fear to despair, from anxiety to hopelessness. There are others whose zest for living has dwindled from high purpose and meaning to arid endurance if not actual futility. The necessity for keeping our attention so long fixed on wars-in-being, and on the worse specter of impending wars, has exacted its price, and few there are among us who do not need help in finding the way through the shadows of threatened global death up the summit of faith and hope.

In this crisis there are people who tell us once again that enough of the right kind of education holds the key to releasing man from his ghastly condition. Although at this moment we have more educational facilities than at any time in our national history, we must still conclude that knowledge is not the same as salvation. Currently there is rather general reliance on the psychiatrist and other psychological consultants to salvage society through individual and group therapy. Yet mental breakdowns outdistance the healing of personalities. With the highest proportion ever of the American population now affiliated with organized religion, little reason can be found for feeling assured that in our religious institutions as presently conducted people are finding resources with which to confront peril to body and soul.

I am convinced that through genuine fellowship we can learn to know the joys of emotional and spiritual health. Fellowship means recognition and appreciation of the worth of our fellows, full-blown sympathy which evokes our disposition to contribute selflessly to them even as we receive from them their regard, their affectionate ministrations. Much of the sense of rootlessness and vacuity that pervades our lives would be dispelled were we to give sufficient thought to the issue of identifying ourselves with the vitality and riches awaiting us in group living: in family, neighborhood, community, and church. It is in these groups that every wholesome personality, every religiously mature person finds that he can recover the meaning of that ancient phrase " the communion of saints."

What the sociologists refer to as primary groups — family, neighborhood, play groups, and the like — contain psychic values which contribute to one's sense of being wanted. For the sake of human growth, primary groups ought to be infused with an educative and spiritual purpose. It is up to religiously motivated people to show how this might be done. Although religion derives its significance from communion, organized religion suffers from a lack of fellowship sufficient for its own needs, to say nothing of the larger problem of supplying enough fellowship for the revitalizing of family, neighborhood, and community. Yet there must be a way for a spiritual communion to proceed to nurture persons in their social groups.

It is for this reason that this book is written. On some of these pages suggestions are to be found for taking the Church out of its sociological classification as a secondary group —

where, unfortunately, it now belongs — and making it a body of primary groups. My hope is that parents, teachers, lawyers, doctors, ministers, and other workers will find incentive for doing just that.

In the initial preparation of this manuscript I was stimulated by the interest of my colleagues at Andover Newton Theological School and by the generous observations of Professor Nels F. S. Ferré, formerly a member of the Andover Newton faculty. In the final stages of writing, I have received particular help from my family and detailed guidance from Dr. Paul L. Meacham, Religious Books Editor of The Westminster Press, whom I heartily thank. My thanks too are due Dr. Paul Hutchinson, outstanding editor and helpful friend, for permission to use parts of Chapters 5 and 6, which first appeared in *The Christian Century*.

WESNER FALLAW.

INTRODUCTION

For a long time I had thought to write a book on the theme of security for today. Surely the need for further attention to the problem of insecurity would justify this attempt. There followed a dialogue in my mind which can be summarized in this way:

Question: What do you mean by security?

Answer: Let's come at it indirectly. Suppose we consider the meaning of insecurity.

Question: Can we say that insecurity is the fear or anxiety that fastens on a disturbed person's life?

Answer: Yes. The fearful or anxious person is emotionally upset, and he may suffer from religious uncertainty, doubt, or even spiritual agony. Always he is in some degree disquieted within himself. Though he may not know it, the chances are that he is unable to love fully because he has experienced too little love. His insecurity is a kind of emotional and spiritual sickness that very likely can be traced back to childhood, when he felt that his parents deprived him of proper affection, respect, and trust. A deprived child senses that he is unwanted and soon he considers himself unworthy. In his unhappiness he may turn against himself. Why not? No one seems to value him. The reason must be, he feels, that he is no good and therefore deserves to be neglected and punished for his hostile feelings and bad deeds. The anxious, insecure person continues in the adult years to punish himself by imagined fears. As a result he is unable to grow into maturity.

Question: Are you saying that an insecure adult always has a history of unloving parents?

Answer: At least the parents did not love wisely. In one way or another they were doubtless inadequate persons. Over and over again such fathers and mothers are found to be immature, and perhaps socially and vocationally incompetent. Almost always the fault is not theirs alone, for they, like their child, are victims of a chain of personal and social relations (and possibly economic conditions) that leave them in need of sympathy and help. Assuredly they are not to be censured.

Question: Then you imply that the victim of insecurity has become disturbed, not from a simple cause, but from a complex of circumstances.

Answer: Exactly. It seems fair to say that an unloving, distrustful, frightened person is the product of many failures — some due to his childhood home, others due to his community, his neighborhood, and his church.

Question: Do you overlook the failure of the schools? And what about a social order that today boasts of many psychological clinics and other agencies designed to help persons to grow into mature adult life?

Answer: No, I do not overlook the schools, nor the social agencies, nor the thousands of professional workers who are attempting to help persons to attain maturity and intelligent citizenship. Modern education is doing more than at any time in human history to deal with individuals according to their psychological needs. Society now offers greater facilities for psychiatric diagnosis and cure than has hitherto been the case. The situation is both ironical and tragic. It is as though people were starving in the midst of plenty, for all those who are emotionally and spiritually insecure are starving amidst our educational, psychological, and religious resources.

Question: What is your answer to this appalling issue? Another book on psychological therapy?

Answer: No. In the first place, that task belongs to the professional psychological consultant. And in the second place, genuine security is achieved only as one finds his way into spiritual maturity. This is a major concern of the exponent of religion. As a religious educator, I have invested some years with groups and individuals with the purpose in mind to work with them toward spiritual maturity.

Question: Then you essay, do you not, a larger task than that of the psychiatric worker who aims to guide a person from emotional inadequacy into psychological maturity?

Answer: Yes. But I too am much concerned with maturity. Let me be explicit about this. I believe that the kind of maturity that really stands up is greater than the maturity confined to the emotions and the intellect. It includes the whole person and is the core of his life. It springs from his heart, from his devotions to God as well as to man. This maturity is possible only as the horizon of the human spirit envisions life now as but an aspect of a larger life. In short, maturity is attained by the person who responds in love to the God of time and eternity who confronts man. Indeed, I do not find maturity evidenced by people who are unable to trust in God and experience love for him at least as decidedly as they love themselves and hold their fellows in affectionate regard.

Question: Granted that spiritual maturity is something over and above the maturity about which the psychologists of personality speak, is the religious educator trying to say that certain psychologists and psychiatrists are deceiving people into thinking that they can know security if only they will become socially adjusted and emotionally stable?

Answer: Let's not talk about psychologists and psychiatrists in terms of what we think they believe personally. Some of them rely on God's healing work no less than on the science and art of therapy. It is to these that we may well look for valid help when a degree of insecurity deepens into pervasive fears that take their toll in psychotic anxiety. But I think that we should consider any psychological and any psychiatric worker as but one member of a team of human servants ready to offer therapy to persons sick in heart and sick in soul. We must remember that this team also includes the physician of the soul who takes his cues from the Great Physician. The psychiatrist, the minister, the teacher, the counselor, and the parent, all ought to hold two clear-cut views about what is required to help persons to achieve maturity, as a requisite for spiritual security. The first view is that growth of human personality entails the combined service of a team of servants who are, in the best sense of the word, ministers. And the second view is that each servant who is wholly dedicated to the delicate and sacred task of aiding persons in becoming what they have been endowed to be must see himself as but a helper of the Creator.

Question: Are you saying that God is always at the center of the process whereby persons achieve maturity and thus become secure?

Answer: Yes.

Question: Therefore, the purpose you have in writing this book could not be adequately set forth by use of the title " Security for Today."

Answer: It could not. Hence the title, TOWARD SPIRITUAL SECURITY.

Question: By this, I take it, you express the hope that the contents to follow point toward personal growth that makes people genuinely secure. Is that your hope?

Answer: It is. I am trying to clarify the issues as to how the individual learns and grows through his basic group relations. The individual and his need for spiritual wholeness is in the forefront of my thought. At the outset in these chapters I try to show him in his social contexts and indicate how the community, the neighborhood, the family, and the church may educate him and foster his development toward maturity. Then I offer some case material from the counseling room, where I have sought to give intensive help to the troubled person who aspires to grow spiritually.

Throughout these pages I draw upon education, psychology, and religion in an effort to develop the thesis that a person can be secure only to the degree that he enjoys whole (wholesome) relations with his fellows, and, accordingly, grows into the maturity of a spiritual personality. The way to wholeness of personality, to holiness of heart, is, finally, one and the same; and it leads to spiritual security.

Question: Since you write as a religious educator, are you going to show the central place that the church must occupy in guiding the family and the community in their educational ministry to individuals and groups?

Answer: That is my intention. Now let me get on with this Introduction.

The Church is a fellowship of people bound together by a common love of God and by mutual regard and affectionate service for one another. But because it is often more human than divine in its values and conduct, the Church frequently bears little resemblance to a body of persons gathered in love to enjoy the fruits of the Spirit. Love, joy, peace, forbearance take flight and the Body of Christ is left anemic if not desiccated. How, then, can the Church exercise its work of effective education and ministry to the hungry and lonely spirits of men?

I see the Protestant Churches of America severely handicapped largely because they have not been so successful as they might be in developing the vital human relations required of a genuine fellowship. The Church must enable the Holy Spirit to dwell among men, and demonstrate the allegiance of person to person, of person to group. Toward these ends the churches can learn to use better ways in nurturing children and adults. They can advance to participate effectively with family and community where men and women are struggling to be good parents and worthy neighbors and citizens. This volume presents some of the steps in an educational and spiritual advance.

The religious leader and the layman alike are concerned with exploring the meaning of fellowship and its promise of contributing emotional stability and spiritual security to individuals and to society. Many people feel themselves trapped and helpless before a tide of personal and world events that seems destined to destroy the individual's last degree of freedom. Fate rather than freedom of choice appears to be real. Taught from childhood to believe in the individual's right and privilege to be both self-directive and influential in shaping the course of history, people today lean toward the pessimistic conviction that freedom is dead and blind fate is astride a careening universe. This sharp change in fundamental belief is so shocking as to corrode some personalities and to crush others. Hence the widespread dissipation of hope for a better human order by means of education, good will, reason, and democracy. Hence too the pitiable incidence of personality disintegration.

But the truth is that the possibility remains for the individual's achieving a wholesome personality (psychological integration), and a mature religious personality (spiritual wholeness). Babies continue to be born with the possibility for good no less than for evil. It is still true that children are endowed from birth with the impulse to grow, the urge to learn, the desire to achieve the values and status that the people close to them may evidence in daily conduct. Youth continue to identify themselves with heroes, and by means of spiritual nurture in home, community, and church, they will elect as their heroes persons of religious stature.

Religious personality has never been handed to people as a gift from heaven. In any time, in any situation, the individual has had to strive for the quality that could lift him above savagery, egoism, provincial-mindedness, and personal pride. It is historic fact that even hardened adults could experience radical transformation from sinful existence and stand before their fellows made new. In times past some of the chiefest of sinners attained saintliness. So now, even in our materialistic culture, men can be set free to experience the life of the spirit. But they must meet the conditions imposed by the process of gaining freedom. Two things are necessary: first, the individual shall move decisively toward spiritual maturity; and, second, he must relate himself intimately and reciprocally with his fellows in family, neighborhood, and church.

When a person does these two things consistently and intelligently, he will discover that no one is religiously mature who either claims that human values are adequate for the good life or that all responsibility for the course of a man's life depends solely on God. He will perceive that spiritual security is invariably denied anyone who disregards the basic fellowship groups and retreats into the isolation of selfish irresponsibility. He will know that the person who nurses the illusion that he is free to do as he pleases thereby arrests his growth toward security, if indeed he escapes enslaving anxiety or psychotic and spiritual destruction.

Joined with his kind, and bound by the spirit of human and divine fellowship, the person who so chooses can gain freedom. In this freedom there is spiritual security for all who diligently seek it and, having found it, reverently nourish it.

1

COMMUNITY FELLOWSHIP

❦ ❦

THE FATE of man and his world hangs in doubt. Informed people know quite well that a third world
war may bring chaos, and write *finis* to civilization. Not
only so; because American life has long tended toward individualism, this development has reached such an extreme
that, were there no need to fear world destruction, there
would still be need for man to change his condition of loneliness and uneasy isolation.

Man is so made as to be unable to endure extreme separate-
ness from his kind. He was made for community; his whole
being suffers when the course of his life prevents his having
abundant interaction with a family, a neighborhood, a community. Emotional security depends ultimately upon religious security wherein one is convinced that he may enjoy a
continuing and dependable relationship both with his Creator and with his kind. No man is ever truly secure save as he
experiences genuine community, and to experience community means that a person communes with his fellows.
This communion is indispensable, for by means of it persons
give back and forth to each other their attention, their consideration, affection, mutual helpfulness, and love. To live
means that persons must give and receive from each other.
To be denied the vitalizing experience of giving and receiving attention and affection is to be denied life, for mere
existence is all that is left.

When his world seems friendly and stable, a man may get along fairly well somewhat alone, with little interaction with others. But when perils crowd in, even the solitary type of person, who ordinarily subsists happily alone, suddenly feels acute need for communion. Modern life demands communion. Men crave fellowship which issues from persons communing one with another. Face-to-face dealings, in which men share thought and feeling, fears and hopes, are essential to emotional and spiritual health. It cannot be stressed too much that personal security, in psychological and spiritual terms, depends on the sustaining and enriching values that can come only to a person who knows the warmth of fellowship within a community which accepts him, gives him his place, and at the same time receives from him that which he has to give. Created for fellowship — which means the capacity to appreciate and enrich the worth of his several fellows — man, in his impersonal urbanized existence, has sought to do without the communion for which his very soul now cries out in desperate loneliness. Sometimes his desperation falters and withers into despair and he retreats into psychotic oblivion. If he is stronger, he resorts, unconsciously protective of himself, to neurosis. That is man today — the neurotic, devoid of neighborliness, bereft of community fellowship, therefore unready for and incapable of religious fellowship.

Organized religion exerts so little influence on modern man precisely because he is a despairing isolate unfit for spiritual communion. Generally speaking, before the masses can be reached for the nurture of religion they have to be incorporated into community, neighborhood, and home group experiences wherein they might be made fit for the larger experience of religious communion. We need to know how persons experience fellowship, and thus derive social and emotional security, basic to experiencing spiritual security within the Christian fellowship, the Church. In some of these chapters the group is brought into focus; in the rest, our concern is with the individual — and how he can be helped to become a spiritually secure person, both in crisis and during ordinary times.

Fellowship when experienced involves communion where you live. Social poise, the sense of well-being, of being wanted, of contributing to your loved ones in home and community, all equip you for the larger experiences that inhere in the company of believers, the Church. So, also, if you are already enjoying communion with fellow religionists, you will inevitably carry this same quality of fellowship into your relationships at home and among your neighbors. Everyone who enjoys social and emotional security with his fellows outside the Church advances a step toward readiness for full spiritual security in the Church, which is valid security, the kind that is requisite for confronting the crisis of our times as well as for dealing maturely with personal problems during ordinary times.

I

What is fellowship in community? In his chapter "War and the Human Community," in the symposium *Learning and World Peace,* Baker Brownell makes the sage comment that in a community " people can know each other as whole persons." This statement suggests that the minute you find yourself using Mr. X as a golf partner, Mr. Y as a repairman, Mr. Z as a specialist in something else, and so limit your regard and contacts with these men, you know that you have reduced human relations to fractions. Your interest in people thus becomes not complete but partial communication. Instead of having persons around you with whom to exchange viewpoints about the major issues that concern you and them, you have bits of expression back and forth. Instead of communion with persons, you have barter with human beings who are but utilities — to help you to play golf, to repair your machinery, and so forth. Reduction of persons to the status of utilities prevents human relations from becoming organic and makes life mechanistic and impersonal. Impersonal relations, when widely practiced, kill man's sense of belonging. And not to know that we belong to our fellows and they to us, not to give and receive warm acceptance and to experience mutual concern for human well-being, is to suffer uncertainty and to doubt that we have social rootage or adequacy, perhaps to fear that we lack intellectual competence or emotional stability. No man in this condition can be secure. Yet most of life in our society is reduced to fractional relations, and because of this we pay a price.

Brownell says that " a community is a group of neighbors who know each other. It is a face-to-face or primary group " (p. 341). Common needs and similar values — standards by which to conduct business, recreational, religious, and cultural affairs — have always served to draw people together in community. Pioneers found need to help one another to clear the wilderness, fight the enemy, build houses, harvest crops. Education and religion fostered community in early America until a generation or two ago. But with the decline of rural society came industrialization and urbanization, with large-scale enterprises that developed a money economy which caused people to buy goods and services — once provided by the family and by larger groups — instead of bartering them by verbal agreement. This changed situation has drastically curtailed face-to-face relations and has reduced life from fellowship to relative isolation. Impersonal systems have been erected only to stifle personal agreement, and the result is that creativity has been largely swallowed up by mass activity. The situation is symbolized by ready-made suits of clothes, standardized canned goods, chain stores, gigantic manufacturers, multiple housing, absentee ownership, and the whole managerial system. The colossus that we call modern society leaves us lonely, cloaked in anonymity, most of us the proverbial cog in the machine — which means that we are but separate mechanisms. It is so difficult to find human warmth amidst the chill of this kind of existence that we have been forced to resort to synthetic warmth induced by scurrying hither and yon to places where sports and other diversions dull our sense of lostness for a purchasable period of time.

Fellowship, as a human relationship in which persons value each other and express mutual regard, appreciation, concern, and helpfulness, makes community possible, and in turn it arises in community. Fellowship and community are two sides of the same coin; or, they may be said to be the light and dark of a complete day.

Like much of life today, fellowship has moved toward institutionalization and specialization. Because of the stiff and tense tempo at which we live, we have striven to maintain fellow feelings by setting aside particular times under especially designated organizational auspices in order to have fellowship one with another. So it is that representatives of labor, management, professional groups, and other organizations journey great distances at stated times for sessions of their various national fellowships, to which their local chapters are related. Local chapters cut across neighborhood and community lines and absorb about all the remaining time that members can spare, thus prohibiting experiences of neighborliness which their members might otherwise have in their home communities. A man often knows members of his fellowship across the country better than he knows the people in the next apartment. But proper valuation of persons requires time spent together, continuous personal cultivation, and generous sharing of needs, hopes, and aspirations. Like the humanitarian who is generally prodigal with his service save when directed toward his own family, too many of us try to anchor our loyalties in widely and thinly spread undertakings, to the detriment of the community where our home is and where our children are growing up.

Burgess and Locke's monumental work *The Family* takes into account the mobility of American life. Before World War II city families moved about once every three years, but during mobilization and wartime people move even more as they throng to industrial centers, and migrate from one part of the country to another. In normal times more than half the population lives in rented apartments, and now home ownership continues to lag. More than other countries, ours is one with people on the move, who do not stay in a community long enough to become identified with it, who suffer the consequences of being free from restraints which neighbors normally impose upon each other. You can be sure that you are experiencing community when what your neighbors say about you matters, makes a difference to you, holds you in check, or causes you to glow with realization of belonging to the neighborhood, caring about its people, and contributing to the common good. This feeling means that you have rootage, spiritual and psychic nourishment indispensable to well-being. But this is precisely what an enlarging proportion of Americans lack. Mutuality, co-operation, face-to-face contacts, common habits and attitudes within family and society — all of which spell communion among persons — are blocked out because of large-scale national and world changes.

Even the strongly flowing tide toward the social welfare state — though on the whole desirable and necessary — contributes to the destruction of community. No one can be sure whether the functions of the Federal Government — in education, medical care, old-age pensions, provision for jobs during economic emergency, and the like — will eventually complete the rout of community or spread it to the outer reaches of the United States and a larger section of the world. What is clear is that there is both threat and hope to be found in enlargement of responsibility on the part of the Government for the welfare of all the people. We must keep in mind, however, that though genuine community is a worthy goal for the nation and the world, its components must be relatively small areas — neighborhoods and towns — in which individuals may know and value each other as they solve their common problems. Our problem is the twofold one of co-operative living in compassable units — geographical and spiritual neighborhoods — and spreading the nature of the small community to embrace national and international life.

II

Whatever a given community may lack by way of humanitarian and service institutions, it is bound to comprise families, neighborhoods, schools, and churches. Libraries, welfare agencies, medical and psychological clinics, and many other organizations may be considered basic to taking care of modern man. But it is next to impossible to unify community organizations and services so that the whole makes a clear pattern. More important and more regrettable, despite the ideal definition and meaning of community, as matters actually work out, most communities are so loosely knit, so much a patchwork, that the individual often gets caught in tricky crevices lying between the numerous agencies that compose his community. People still endure hunger in the midst of abundant food, still perish amidst community resources and institutions that can marshal all the wisdom of learning and grace of religion. Americans are not much different from the high-caste Indian, who walks unperturbed along crowded village streets where men and women are dying from lack of food and medical care. Though we are appalled by callous conduct in foreign countries, we are often oblivious to human needs in our home community — save that we establish professional agencies and give money to see that people are cared for by remote control. If we are to walk over the bridge of neighborliness and live in community as persons imbued with fellowship, as persons conscious of man's nature and God's design for human destiny, we shall have to take bold steps on our own.

Opportunities to do just this are repeatedly offered us. For example, your grammar school boy comes home with a new friend. At the age of ten the visitor can outtalk, outsmart, outappeal most adolescents and many adults. You are charmed and troubled by his undue craving for attention, for affection, for security. The story comes out during the next weeks and months as your child and his new friend visit back and forth. Most of the visiting is done in your home because young Bill's home cannot hold him or attract playmates.

Bill is an only child of parents who married in mid-life. His mother is in and out of hospitals most of the time, and though his father tries hard, he is too old and troubled to understand a ten-year-old. Bill is not at all neglected so far as food, shelter, and clothing are concerned, but he wants to be loved, to belong. What is missing in his home he attempts to compensate for by tall tales about what he and his father do together, and what he and his mother are going to do when she gets well. Meantime he begins to conduct himself in a manner that lets you know why it is that he loses friends as quickly as he gains them. He does not know how to play with his peers, for he is too aggressive and too demanding. When something goes wrong, he always blames the other child. At an age when he should have outgrown childish falsehoods, he lies in a most convincing fashion. He gets into fights, as often as he can manage, with smaller children; he hits and runs from boys his size. He tries to buy companionship by passing out candy and other treats. How does he get hold of so much money? You learn at a Parent-Teacher Association meeting that none of the parents any longer permit Bill to come to their homes and they try to keep their children from him at school. The fifth grade teacher tells you, in a private talk, that the school psychologist, the principal, and the minister of the church where Bill goes to Sunday school have been unable to accomplish anything by talking with the boy. Rumor has it that the father once asked the minister to deal with Bill, to stop his pilfering and lying, but the teacher does not know what, if anything, came of this request.

You begin to be glad that Bill does not live in your immediate neighborhood and you are relieved that your older children are getting tired of his coming to your home and imposing on their ten-year-old brother. Brother too says that though he feels sorry for Bill he is going to punch him on the nose if he keeps on acting like a dictator. But for some reason Bill never quite fades from sight. Besides, he is getting indelibly stamped on your conscience, for Bill is a lost soul. He needs help, not shunting from agency to agency. And the child has possibilities, for he responds to affection like the children in the orphan home where in your youth you led recreation and told stories. Furthermore, you reason, Bill's family is a part of your community. The child and his parents are suffering from inattention. Are the parents approachable?

The father was approachable after his wife's final visit to the hospital. As soon as you heard the news, you went over and found him, a man nearly old enough to be your father, trying to get supper for himself and Bill. While you and he talked, you helped to set the table and prepare the food. And in the months that followed he and Bill dined occasionally with your family. He was finding help from a psychiatrist at the family clinic, learning how to think and feel as Bill thinks and feels. The Social Service Bureau finally located a competent housekeeper for the home. As program chairman of the P.T.A., you secured two or three speakers whom you were sure could speak to the condition of Bill and his father.

Now the accumulated results of your human investment begin to be clear, and you realize that other parents of Bill's classmates are aware of a change in the boy. One of the fathers has helped Bill to improve his skill in baseball. At school and in the neighborhood the boys begin to include him in their games. Bill and his father are seen by the neighbors going off together on fishing trips. You hear that though Bill formerly knew all the answers and caused more disturbance at Sunday school than the rest of the class combined, he now talks less and co-operates more. Nor does he fail to inform the fellows that his dad has been made an officer in the men's club of the church.

Thinking over what you may have contributed to Bill and his father (and what they have contributed to you), you draw up a list of working principles which you believe point toward practical community fellowship:

1. One may not *assume* that he is his brother's keeper. He *is*.

2. Holding back when a human need is apparent cannot be excused by saying "those people will think I'm a busybody."

3. Agencies may be futile without the help of a concerned neighbor.

4. If adults designate a troublesome child as "a bad boy," exclude him from their homes, and try to keep their children from him, they give him another push toward possible delinquency and ruin.

5. A citizen ought at least to be as alert for opportunity to render help in the name of humanity, in the name of a loving God, as he is for a good buy at a bargain counter.

6. Every community has its quota of human needs, of forgotten people for lack of whose fellowship the community suffers.

7. Bill's conduct definitely was what the child psychologists call symptomatic of his actual inner nature.

8. Before Bill could profit from guidance his home had to have help.

9. Even today adults in surprising numbers do not know how to go about getting help either for their children or for themselves.

10. Bill's father was teachable. Adults can learn when they are properly motivated.

11. Undoubtedly one of the persons who was most helped by your venture was your own child, whom you saved from learning to look upon young Bill with disfavor or unwarranted superiority.

12. To live in community means to communicate. Can this permit any blocking off of any persons?

13. Community welfare, human well-being, is the concern of anybody — anybody who perceives that serving his neighbor requires far more than willingness to take the time and to exercise tact, and far more than ability to enjoy human encounter: it takes personal fitness which can be derived only from willingness and capacity to be helped, whether need for help is at first recognized or not.

Clearly children reveal the quality of homes from which they come, and homes are an accurate index of the community in which they are established. So, also, the community lastingly influences the lives of children who learn not only the values of their several families but also the standards of their particular community. Using children as the index to the story of America, we are forced to conclude that much remains to be accomplished before many of our communities attain merit that warrants the ideal contained in Brownell's definition. According to data gathered by Frances M. Cushing for the United Council of Church Women, less than half of America's nearly fifty million children under eighteen years of age have the benefit of the kind of homes, health, and education necessary for their proper development. Mrs. Cushing has compiled facts which show that presently one in twenty children born annually will, at some time in life, require and receive care in mental hospitals. These children of economically rich America evidently come from socially and psychologically impoverished communities where the stability and nurture of genuine community are missing. Fellowship, the quality that makes persons into a community, is lacking, and therefore community life as most of us find it is far from being a primary group experience essential to fruitful adult life and productive of whole relationships needed for nurturing children.

As we observe the people where we live, we assess the human resources that foster or negate personal and social security. Persons who characteristically reach out toward us and communicate their thoughts, hopes, and desires with respect to the welfare of our community bespeak their concern for their fellows, their desire to share with them opportunities and responsibilities for strengthening community. Only so can a neighborhood, a town, or a city provide its citizens with resources equal to the task of overcoming the tendencies so widespread today that make good community relations impossible.

Certain communities seem to have more than their share of people who are outgoing in attitude toward their fellow townsmen — who possess the disposition and talent for developing neighborliness. Towns like this attract us; we want to be near people who are genuinely cordial and friendly. Close observation enables us to take at least a rough measure of the kind of people where we live; and well we may take their measure, for it is people first, last, and always upon whom the quality of community depends.

III

If you are considering moving to a new community, you have the opportunity to make a choice based on Christian ethical standards. Few people do so, and because of this the whole social order suffers.

Transportation makes possible a wider range of choices of places to live than was true a generation ago. Despite a continuing housing shortage, a family may be able to select its community according to desired resources and institutions. A young father was explaining what he and his wife were looking for in suburban New York: a simple house, with a yard for the children to play in, within walking distance of grocery stores, modern schools, a church, and neighbors from different racial backgrounds. The last qualification was underscored, for this father believes in Christianity and democracy rooted in intercultural experiences. So it was that he and his family moved to a street where Negroes, Orientals, Jews, and Gentiles mingle on the basis of personal worth. This is a neighborhood in which intercultural and interfaith education is taking place as children and adults grow in respect, appreciation, and helpfulness toward each other. How does such a community operate? What happens to persons within it?

Its white children, who are in the majority, will play as naturally with black and brown and yellow children as they do with other white children — in so far as the parents of all these children inculcate in them, during their preschool years, unbiased attitudes and behavior; for children absorb, imitate, and adopt the attitudes and conduct of their parents. These are the years during which the families from varying racial backgrounds should visit back and forth freely, sharing life as fully as personal affinity warrants, solely on the basis of human worth. False or strained relationships will defeat the purpose, however sincere, that parents have to engage in democratic and ethical experiences with neighbors of many colors and creeds.

When the children start to school, even one whose leadership is committed to democracy and intercultural guidance, parents will be alert to counteract the inevitable influences toward prejudice and discrimination. Even in the most positively committed democratic school, factors are present that work to undermine interracial fellowship. Young Jim comes in one day from school saying that the fellows tell him he ought not to invite black Sally to his birthday party, as he always has done up to now. Jane informs her mother that her neighbor, six-year-old Isaac, and his parents are strange people. She has heard this from a classmate whose father never employs Jews in his business. But democratic homes, working with a democratic school, can survive threats of discrimination until the children reach adolescence. When young people begin dating, they generally start excluding persons of different skin color and religions. Yet some hold fast to democracy, to fellowship, maintaining fellowship across the barriers of prejudice. For this they and their parents pay a price.

Persons who depart from custom have to expect criticism

and difficult adjustments to delicate issues. When nineteen-year-old Susan gets serious about her brown boy friend with whom she has played all her life, the real test of human worth has to be faced, even though the families of both have lived in neighborly regard. When young Jacob announces that he and Ann, his childhood Gentile playmate, are going to be married, his orthodox Jewish parents will have to re-examine their conflicting religious and democratic allegiances.

The people who object to intermingling of families on a community level are correct when they foresee intermarriage as a possible ultimate outcome of democratic idealism in practice. They are consistent in their convictions when they oppose junior high school mixed dancing, with children of different races mingling on a social level as they do on an educational level. They are also consistent when they seek to live as far away from other races as possible and prefer separate schools. Though they break up community into discriminatory bodies which refuse to practice democracy, they are true to their thoroughgoing biases. On the other hand, many avowedly democratic people inconsistently foster democratic fellowship through neighborhood, school, and community relations, only to destroy all they have worked for when intermarriage becomes a likelihood for a member of their own family.

When Ann's parents learned that she loved Jacob and wanted to marry him, they discussed her feelings with her just as they had always talked through things together. Ann understood that Jewish-Gentile marriages add many more problems to the making of a successful home. Because she was intelligent, and her thinking not clouded over by emotional fights with parents who might have acted unreasonably when she told them of her love for Jacob, she was able

to make a calm appraisal of the chances for a happy marriage. And she was ready to go ahead with it, until Jacob's
parents, in the name of their religion, forced him to break
the engagement. Ann was no more wounded than Jacob, and
both of them bowed to what seemed unavoidable. They
could have gone ahead with their plans, but each had always
believed that marriage, to be secure, needs foundations of approval that only the families of the bride and groom can
provide. At length Ann and Jacob, independently of each
other, recognized in themselves something that neither cared
to admit to anyone: a sense of relief that they would not
have to face bringing up children who might never be able
to identify themselves with either Jewish or Gentile cultural
patterns. Nevertheless, each would have gone ahead with the
marriage had their families supported them, knowing that
some Jewish-Gentile homes build secure family and community relations.

It is noteworthy that community relations seem to provide
greater fellowship for minority groups when they are a small
minority than when they are large. When clannishness develops and people flock together along racial lines, interracial
and interfaith communing is curtailed. Exclusiveness promotes antipathies, and lack of understanding based largely
on misinformation. Groups narrowly grounded in race or
religion tend to pit group against group, and thus weaken
or destroy a sense of community. This situation imperils democracy, impoverishes intercultural education, and increases
insecure feelings which issue in aggressiveness on the part of
individuals.

There are those who believe that America's minority problems will never be settled until racial amalgamation through
gradual intermarriage is accomplished. But meantime social
amalgamation need not await racial and cultural amalgama-

tion. And social amalgamation is simpler when families of
minority groups choose to live in communities where they
are greatly outnumbered. For being outnumbered induces
them to seek fellowship with the majority even as they find
themselves relatively acceptable because they are not numerous enough to represent a threat to the majority. Conscious
or unconscious adoption of local community customs facilitates identification with the majority.

But utter conformity to prevailing social, religious, and
cultural patterns is not suitable for establishing a democratic
community and providing individuals with emotional and
spiritual security; surrender of fundamental beliefs and customs is not the answer to the problem of establishing fellowship within our communities. Experiences in neighborhood
groups and interrelationships among these groups throughout the community make possible cross-fertilization, growth
of a hybrid community, which results in corporate and personal enrichment. Religiously and sociologically speaking,
persons and their institutions ought not to seek to conform,
but rather to be transformed by the renewing of their minds
according to standards of truth higher than those afforded
by separated cultures with their particular customs and
values.

If we choose a homogeneous community in which to live
we thereby circumscribe our family's development; we restrict ourselves to the customs and standards of " our kind of
people " instead of reaching for the larger values found in
intercultural and interracial fellowship. Choosing a community, like choosing a marriage companion, is a crucial matter. On it depends the growth of persons and the realization
of social values, democratic or undemocratic.

Nevertheless people who deliberately project their families
into communities of mixed races and religions should know

what they are undertaking. They are incurring social hazards which may defeat them emotionally and spiritually. For propinquity among children of mixed heritages and values means abandonment of any parental desire to be at ease. Only through moral and religious fortification of unusual merit can persons intelligently and satisfactorily solve the problems cited above which typify relations among young people who grow up together in a mixed community.

Both democracy and Christianity demand of us, not retreat, but a positive approach to ethical controversy and moral difficulty. It is in the nature of persons of both faiths (democracy and Christianity) to work through human problems toward goals and satisfactions that can be reached only by persons who give themselves altruistically to human need, suffering to reach ideals unattainable save as comfortable isolation and deceptive complacency are abandoned. Persons dedicated to honoring God by serving man quite understand that to gain life they may not seek first their own security from social and personal problems; rather, they know that their spiritual security lies through the daring and arduous task of working out within their own community the intricate problem of reconciling the differences and suspicions and hatreds that set cultural groups against each other. Dedicated persons must be willing to lose their social status, if not their lives, so that they can truly find themselves, and thus be at one with themselves and the God of all being.

IV

Among educators there is a growing demand that public schools shall become community schools and serve all the people, adults as well as children. Interest groups that include hobby clubs, mental and manual skills, artistic and social development are being provided in increasing numbers.

Afternoon and evening schools often serve youth and older people in ways as manifold and varied as interests require. Homer Kempfer, reporting in *School and Society* (Volume 68, September 11, 1948), says that a Gallup Poll in December, 1944, found that 34 per cent of all adults wished to continue their education, and a July, 1947, poll found that 41 per cent wanted more education. The Gallup findings have been substantiated by other surveys. Twenty-five years ago the studies of E. L. Thorndike reversed the general opinion that adults can learn little. As a matter of fact, we know that much of the creative intellectual work of the world is done by people of middle age and beyond. What adults intend to learn they generally can learn under normal circumstances. When interest and need are present, accomplishment will follow.

Adult classes may well be related to the public school, though organized labor, character-building agencies, churches, and other institutions are also engaged in adult education. However, the school is peculiarly equipped either to sponsor and promote classes or to house those established and conducted by other agencies. The school is there, paid for by tax money, with facilities that can be used at a cost little higher than the figure at which they are operated for children. Moreover, the school is nonpartisan, and therefore provides opportunity for people to gather under favorable circumstances. It is neutral territory which labels no one who enters it.

Leaders in the multiplying adult education classes of the nation ought to aim at experimentation in community good will and co-operation. Any goal less worthy is unsuitable to the needs of our day.

Social growth, community development, stems from emotionally and spiritually emancipated persons — persons who have been released from the suspicion and resentment, fear and hatred that cling to the best men among us who avow that they seek to live democratically, ethically, and religiously. A study class of adults exploring community institutions and their functions is a suitable setting in which to make use of group therapy through role-playing. This technique comes from specialists engaged in psychodrama and sociodrama, but it can be used in the classroom, as will be seen below.

Sydney is a medical doctor, a young bachelor who is outgoing toward everyone, but who, nevertheless, is so assertive as to irritate people. He overdoes things. All fall he has been attending the Monday night class in Community Institutions. He often tells the other twenty men and women — two or three Jews, a few Catholics, Protestants, and skeptics — that he has seen enough of the failure of churches and synagogues to make him believe that neither religion nor education can cause people to live together as a genuine democratic community. And because he thinks that people really do not commune, as neighbors and friends, Sydney asks how world peace can ever prevail. The man is serious, and he keeps coming back to his searching question. Members of the class offer numerous suggestions, many naïve, some hopeful, others pessimistic. " I would start working in the synagogue tomorrow — or in any church that would guarantee to create a brotherhood — if I had reason to hope for good will among men," the doctor says. He and the teacher, a professor of sociology from a local college, have talked privately several times after class. The professor knows that Sydney's problem of insecurity is chiefly with himself. The professor is speaking:

" What situations arise in which people find it impossible to trust each other? "

Sydney: " I'll give you a typical situation. Last night I was called to a home to treat a new patient. Apparently the wife had telephoned the first doctor whose name she found in the directory. She was excited — thought her husband had had a heart attack. It turned out that it was only a mild stomach upset. Pretty soon I had the old boy eased, and so was his wife — she was so relieved, in fact, that she began to look intently at me while I was writing a prescription. I guess she had no idea at first that I'm Jewish. Sydney Johns could be anybody's name. At any rate, when I offered to call in today — just to double-check on the patient — she assured me that would not be necessary. I left as quickly as I could, and that was that. Today, when I checked up to see who it was I was visiting I found out that the old boy is a Protestant bishop. Could you beat it? No wonder they don't want a Jew in their house. Now how can a man in my position either trust Protestants or believe that any religious institution works to create community values? "

Professor: "Thank you, you've stated — "

But a dozen people interrupt, trying either to support the doctor or to defend the bishop. Finally a housewife, Constance Philips, a perceptive person, is heard saying that Dr. Johns as like as not has completely misjudged the bishop's wife.

Professor: "This seems a good opportunity for Dr. Johns to show us more precisely just what went on during his visit, particularly the latter part of it. He will need help; someone will have to be the bishop's wife. This table can be the bishop's bed. Here he is, this book. But we need his wife — a live woman among us."

The doctor asks Mrs. Philips to play the part and proceeds to re-enact his visit of last evening. The professor instructs him to go through all the motions, examining the patient, talking to him and his wife just as he actually did. Constance quickly becomes the agitated patient's wife, fluttering around the bed and praying the doctor to quiet the bishop's moaning. The play moves along remarkably realistically and the class sit absorbed, not missing a point.

Soon the patient rests and the wife grows calm. Only the doctor continues to talk volubly. At one point Constance (as the wife) is moved to ask,

"May we just step over here, doctor? "

Sydney is about to do so when he stops, suddenly staring at Constance. Amazed, he explains to the class that he cannot imagine how Constance could know that the bishop's wife actually did ask him to move away from the bed.

Mrs. Philips: "Of course I did not know what the wife actually did. But if you talked as loudly and as incessantly last night as you've just been doing, I certainly would try to get you to put on the soft pedal."

Gamely the doctor resumes the act, but he breaks in on himself while he is writing the prescription. Constance is staring at him as he writes.

"Please, Mrs. Philips, *don't* look at me that way! "

After the laughter that follows, Constance tells the doctor that anybody in her normal senses would admire the detailed care with which he explains how the medicine is to be taken.

Mrs. Philips: "Furthermore, Dr. Johns, if I may say so — speaking as a happily married woman at least ten years older than you — you are a most presentable specimen of humanity."

The applause is hearty as the participants take their seats and the professor invites the class to discuss the play. As usual Sydney is the first to speak, though everyone is scarcely able to await a turn.

Dr. Johns: "First, I want to thank Mrs. Philips for her flattering remark. Second, I must say that in my opinion she is hardly competent to depict the emotions of a bishop's wife. But she has taught me something about myself that I've never realized before. I talk and talk and talk."

Mrs. Philips: "Loudly."

Dr. Johns: "Yes; I admit it; loudly."

Professor: "In our admiration for Dr. Johns because of his penitent mood, we must not overlook another point that Mrs. Philips made."

Dr. Johns: "No, we mustn't; but she is wrong about the bishop's wife's susceptibility to masculine charm. Anyway, that woman is old enough to be my grandmother."

Mrs. Philips: "I am *not* wrong. Any woman here will tell you that a woman is never too old and never too young to admire a handsome man. What you need, Sydney, is a wife."

Later, when the professor and the doctor were walking down the street, Sydney revealed that he quite understands that he is insecure and that his talkativeness is an effort to hide his feelings. "But tonight I feel better than at any time since I was a kid. I feel as if I'd confessed my sins; a sort of catharsis, you know.

What's more, the class were wonderful to me. I really think I could trust that gang! "

The community school for adults can be enlivened by occasional use of role-playing but certain points should be observed, among which are the following:

1. The story must present an unsolved problem.
2. It might well be one that deeply affects some person who is present and who will play himself.
3. It should be on a theme that members of the group find a common concern.
4. In most cases the person who is selected to play himself should be known to the leader as one who has demonstrated a flair for the dramatic, who rather enjoys the sensation of attracting attention, whose manner, nevertheless, is inoffensive to the group. J. L. Moreno, author of *Who Shall Survive?* and other works, who has developed psychodrama and sociodrama, can look over an audience that may meet only once, and, though the people are unknown to him and to each other, he can select an individual suitable for dramatizing his problem-story. Evidently Dr. Moreno keeps his audience waiting long enough for them to begin chatting among themselves so that he can detect a person who readily becomes the center of conversation of the people seated around him. In most instances such a person will be physically attractive.
5. The problem-story is best depicted after the author (the person with the problem) is given a few minutes with the leader (or his assistant) and the supporting player, during which the highlights of the story are recounted and the incident, or series of incidents, is blocked out by scenes.
6. The author is reminded before and during the role-playing to make clear to the audience where the action is taking place, who was present when the incidents first occurred, and what the circumstances were. The leader helps the author to explain the transitions between scenes. (In the story told above only one scene was depicted. Had the doctor encountered the bishop and his wife on numerous occasions certain happenings would have

been chosen for re-enacting in the play.)

7. No one need bother about dialogue. The author is almost invariably reliable in replaying at least the sense of his conversations that took place in the actual life situation; the supporting player can pick up the essential character and reactions of the person whose part he is playing. During the briefing period preceding the play, the leader and the supporting actor will take care that the author provides adequate information to enable the supporting player to open the play with confidence. As the action develops, the supporting player will readily take his cues from the author-actor.

8. The leader needs to be prepared to step in, to alleviate possibly unbearable tensions that may develop. For example, passages that reveal aspects of a player's life that are too personal may need to be hurried over or deleted. In such instances the leader's function is that of a director-producer, who must decide what is to be cut and then point the way toward the next part of the story. The skillful leader will be able to pick up the main lines of the action without destroying the significance of the story.

9. Properly chosen actors can step out of role, express an aside to indicate that this or that is not a part of the story suitable to reveal, and pass on with the action toward adequate presentation and a definite conclusion.

10. After the play the amount of discussion and evaluation that follows will vary according to the desire of the players and the audience; but the leader reserves the right to restrain the degree and extent of discussion; he will often know that the author-player has taken all he can, emotionally, from the action itself.

11. The playing of a role, when well done, like legitimate theater, may require no further comment. However, the leader will stand ready, if the players so request, to discuss new perspectives gained through role-playing.

12. The insight gained by the author-player may not be the same as the insights that the audience gain. This is unimportant because playing through the problem suffices to release emotions and change the player's attitudes. The way he feels toward himself is probably more important than what the audience think is the solution of his problem.

13. Real-life drama interests the audience because a true story

is being presented. More than that, the audience are interested because familiar situations and problems identical with or close to their own are being resolved. Therapy is taking place both for players and audience — though no one present may be aware of just why he feels so well after the acting is over.

14. The author-player, more than his supporting player and more than the members of the audience, may be expected to be fortified to deal more effectively in everyday human relations. He may actually achieve reorientation of his life; spiritually put, something close to conversion takes place.

15. Release of knotted feelings in persons not only works out individual salvation but sends out into the community persons freed to engage in fellowship not formerly possible for them. Obviously the community will react advantageously to this new force set loose within it.

16. Not everyone engaged in educational leadership should experiment with role-playing. Unlike stage plays, the personal drama is intimate and needs to be handled with particular restraint. The leader must know how to protect persons from injurious revelations. But educators who deal with personal counseling and group guidance have at least some of the necessary qualifications for conducting role-playing.

17. Young people may lend themselves more easily to role-playing than do older people. They are the ones on whom to practice while learning this technique.

18. Older people may need the group therapy of role-playing much more than young people do.

19. Reserved individuals need not be asked to engage in role-playing. The man who sits wrapped in his thoughts, or one who is polite but distant in manner, is seldom a suitable person to undertake role-playing. (The reverse of this is probably true when a skilled therapist is in charge of psychodrama.)

20. The story-problem probably should never be one based on a situation existing between any members of the group; at least no leader less skilled than an expert group therapist (who is a competent psychiatrist) should undertake to present a situation existing witl.in the group.

21. Role-playing may be adapted to a wide variety of family, community, and interpersonal relations.

22. Before undertaking to use this technique a leader ought to have a working knowledge of social psychology, group dynamics, and personal counseling.

23. Extensive practice (preferably as an understudy or an apprentice to a competent group therapist) is needed before a leader may expect to be highly successful in using role-playing. (Even more training is essential if psychodrama is to be attempted with emotionally ill persons.)

V

It is indispensable that one shall commune with his fellows where he lives. Mere communication is not sufficient. To be sure, communicating with others is preliminary to communing with them. But for the sake of his psychological, social, and spiritual well-being, one needs the richer experience of entering fully into the joys, sorrows, successes, and failures of many people in a variety of situations.

When the sense of community breaks down, this means that people in a common geographic and social area have failed to commune together. Physically they may live within reach of one another, but spiritually they are out of touch. Though their paths may cross, they seldom if ever meet and join in a journey of experience together. This state of affairs may go to such an extreme that even the normal communication of acquaintances, who wave to each other in passing or stop to shake hands and chat, breaks down and leaves persons isolated. Extreme isolation engendered by modern urban society plays a considerable part in the prevailing mood which holds that much of the meaning has gone out of life.

Environment is powerfully influential in an individual's development. And because the social community comprises in tangible form a large measure of what is generally meant by environment, we should clearly understand that the community is a very real educative factor in every life within it.

It is in and through primary groups that the individual finds a matrix essential for his growth. The community can be one of these groups. If it is made up of concerned neighbors, of friendly and helpful families, then fellowship as a spiritual quality is made available to persons who without it can never find security or attain spiritual maturity. What the community is to be depends mainly upon the good will, intelligent purpose, and ethical and religious intentions of its people. Two marks of the good community are personal attention to people in need, and continuous growth of adults aided by effective educational groups.

In this chapter we have noted the way in which Bill was restored to happy living, and what this meant to the family that befriended him and his father. In the evening class described above, the young physician learned how to overcome his feeling of being discriminated against and had the experience of entering into rich fellowship with people of a different race.

By careful appraisal of communities, a family may choose to live in one that offers interracial and intercultural communion. There are risks that go with a decision to bring up children in such a community, but if parents honestly and intelligently place more value in democracy and ethical religion, they will find that the risks bring forward greater possibility for community fellowship. And if fellowship is achieved by people of good will within their local community, its chances on the world scene are advanced. Moreover, as individuals are nourished in a constructive environment, where there is a community of ideas and a communion of neighbors, they are being educated for emotional and spiritual maturity. It is the community fellowship that facilitates good family living, prepares people for the greater communion of the Church, and thus counteracts personal insecurity.

2

THE NEIGHBORHOOD: FOSTERING GROUPNESS

❦ ❦

A<small>N</small> E<small>NGLISHMAN</small> commenting on American houses, with doorless living rooms and dining rooms, observes that Americans are a lonely people. As he sees the matter, we do not wish to shut ourselves within our rooms, but rather prefer to be in the middle of all that is going on in the household. The observer concludes that we feel great need for each other. Nevertheless we have allowed ourselves to be swallowed up by big cities. Especially those of us who formerly enjoyed the neighborliness of villages and small towns are apt to lament over city loneliness. Most of us like to be able to call people by name and to have our names called when we walk down the street, but urban life has practically canceled this kind of exchange. Civic clubs, fraternal orders, business-social organizations, labor unions, and the rest are sought for fellowship, as means for our gaining recognition and response, in order to feel that we belong, that we are secure socially. We are inclined to discount the joiner. Rather, we should recognize that the person who attaches himself to every ready organization is hungry for security in fellowship, if not afraid of solitude.

If you are now happily related to a neighborhood group, that group — of whatever kind — can be elevated in purpose and in social and religious effectiveness. Its fellowship need not be confined to recreational and educational values; it can reach beyond customary practices in which individuals

enjoy each other and what they do together, and touch ultimate values inhering in neighborhood groups that are consciously shaping persons for spiritual citizenship. Moreover,
the immediate fellowship can seek to impregnate all life with
the hope that world community may become fit for spiritual
health and human survival. No less goal may be sought if
you are serious about personal security and social salvation.
Each human relationship affects the quality of the neighborhood and each neighborhood affects the whole human order.
No social betterment group should exist as an end within itself; it must always be regarded as a means toward the ultimate end that all men may learn to live more truly, more
positively in keeping with the purpose for which man was
created, more in harmony with the nature of God.

Many people find in their neighborhoods a fellowship that
exceeds that which they experience elsewhere. It is well that
they are related to a group of persons who respect and love
them, who permit full expression, provide support and encouragement and incentive for personal and family and community enrichment. Neighborliness certainly has a religious
quality, and groupness evokes the religious sentiment that
may lead to moral and religious conduct. Whether a primary
group — an intimate, face-to-face relationship — be a family
or a neighborhood club or a church organization, fellowship
can be experienced. Within the group not only recognition
of the worth of persons is realized; more than that, realization of the presence of God is assured, provided the group
experience reaches a level of worship. We shall return to this
in the closing section of this chapter.

Even though few neighborhood groups actually become
worshipful and are not, consequently, assuring persons of
spiritual fellowship superior or even equal to that which may
ordinarily be found in the Christian Church, the argument

still holds that a group of neighbors can experience a real degree of fellowship that sometimes leads to spiritual security. Moreover, if the neighborhood group achieve spiritual fellowship in high degree they come close to being a church. This does not mean that the group members are necessarily attached to a church organization, or that they have formally adopted a creed or systematized their procedures, or laid claim to being a church. In truth, nonconfessionals within the group generally will not be willing to call themselves a part of organized religion. Nor will most confessionals wish to say that their neighborhood group is anything but a fellowship of persons; but genuine fellowship as found within social groups can reflect Christianity. When this is the case, a person may be assured of a group experience in which he gains spiritual security. Whatever one's conclusion about this point may be, it cannot be denied that neighborliness is specific evidence of the fact that those who practice it are headed for spiritual security. The expected outcome of a sense of fellowship is a steady expression of neighborliness. Multiple opportunities are not only needed but are also available to guarantee that neighbors may enjoy spiritual security. It is no more possible for people to live maturely and responsibly without being neighbors than it is for an organism to live without air and water.

I

Granted that the ethical and religious idea of neighborliness is a major clue to security among men and a dominant motif in fellowship, it ought to be rooted in the geographic area: neighborhood. From being too inquisitive about what the neighbors do, much of American society has swung to the opposite pole, where no attention or concern whatever is given to the people around us. Such unrelatedness is indefensible on at least two counts: it denies the basic truth that we are by nature destined to be our brothers' keepers; and it prevents our gaining much-needed experience in practicing the ways of fellowship within small, manageable limits, with the aspiration to permeate all of human society with the genius of group security.

There are numerous and inviting ways to make a start at changing aggregations of people, living in adjoining houses, into neighborhood groups. Perhaps the suburban or small-town community lends itself more readily to neighborhood group life than the city can. Although city life may make no more demands on people for civic, social, and commercial activities than does suburban or small-town life, the fact remains that people who live outside the city are able to be somewhat more leisurely and inaccessible to business demands, therefore freer to cultivate neighborhood interests.

How do groups begin? Among other ways four may be noted:

1. The neighbors of a certain community began to meet in various homes because they liked each other and found common recreational and educational interests. Social enjoyment initially drew them together. Ping-pong and softball, listening to music and making their own music, enabled them to combine play with talkfests. Ordinarily they would not engage in the kind of problem-solving cited in section III of this chapter. But they found that a start on the angle of mutual enjoyment led them naturally to more serious activities.

2. Some neighborhood groups get started by families helping each other as occasions arise. A dentist tells of the custom among his neighbors of wives and husbands preparing for the homecoming of mothers with new babies. In each instance the house is cleaned, the pantry is stocked, food is cooked, flowers are in place. Everybody looks in and does his part. There are times when children are temporarily taken into neighbors' homes, if a mother is sick. When house-painting and repairs are needed, neighbors help

each other. Fellowship is thus developed through group solidarity like that experienced during pioneer days and in an agricultural society.

Helping each other brings people into thinking together, planning together, educating each other in major issues of the day. The group life that grows up informally, around natural needs and in the spirit of helpfulness, does not necessarily lead to regular meetings or systematic group thinking, but it frequently does just that. When you share your bounty or render a service to a neighbor, you make an investment in him. People who practice the art of home cooking still like to run next door with a pie or a jar of jelly. And when death comes to the neighborhood, you find yourself taking care of the bereaved family, looking after their affairs and doing whatever you are prompted by sympathy and love to do. You expand the sense of family so that the neighborhood takes on many of its attributes.

3. When your neighborhood is faced by a problem, that may well be the beginning of group life. In every neighborhood there are persons who serve as rallying points around whom others gather when a common problem needs defining and attacking. The more difficult the problem and the longer people have to spend together in reaching a solution, the better the chances are that a permanent group will develop. If there were more sharing of neighborhood problems, there would very likely be less moving and a greater degree of satisfaction enjoyed by individuals and families. If, for example, street lights are inadequate or garbage disposal irregular, neighbors may get together and compare notes, assessing the extent of their inconvenience. One issue faced together leads to another. After problems, refreshments; and after refreshments, neighborhood picnics. And from being happily together, fellowship develops group life in which productive, corporate action is taken.

4. Children even better than dogs and other pets bring neighbors out of their adult isolation into communication. Far more adults have been introduced to each other by their children than the other way round. We adults will respond to the needs of children in the neighborhood much more readily than to the needs of other adults. But serving the child requires that we serve his parents. The single child next door may be lonely and obviously

in need of child companionship. Your children begin to invite the little neighbor to play with them and to ask you if he may go along with your family for drives in the country. When you ask the child's parents, an acquaintanceship begins that may ripen into friendship. There are people into whose house and yard children of the neighborhood naturally delight to flock. Taking our cue from the children, we adults may profitably begin to flock from one house to the next.

One or two nights a month is not too often for neighbors to spend together. Group solidarity in the neighborhood goes a long way toward eliminating frictions, misunderstanding, and exclusiveness. When you are asked to call on your neighbors for subscriptions to a community fund, you are often impressed with how many interesting people live near you and how little you know them. In a compact suburban residential section, neighborhood groups may be open to families within two or three adjoining blocks. In small towns a group might comprise the people within the radius of a half mile or so. As the group establishes itself, from ten to fifteen couples may constitute the body. Others will probably not be attracted regularly, if at all, because groupness wanes beyond thirty to forty members.

Whatever the beginning of the neighborhood group and its ongoing nature, clublike organization, with officers and bylaws, is to be avoided. The simpler the coming together, the better. Intercultural, interracial, and interfaith groups are quite possible, so long as the children of the neighborhood play together and go to school together. Fellowship across lines that ordinarily divide people is remarkably rewarding within the neighborhood setting.

If there are two or three families in your community who realize that their children stand to gain from parental neighborhood grouping and who know, further, that surprising appreciations and enrichment await those who are willing to experiment with neighborliness around their own doorstep — not confining the idea to Christian foreign missions or the United Nations — then your neighborhood may look forward to a venture in group fellowship. For neighborliness is infectious and a few people so inclined are all that is needed to initiate and guide the development of a neighborhood group in which the individual can experience gratifying security.

II

For those who want to make a careful study of group relations, the following test may be used. The test is in the form of a " groupness report." This report comes from Professor Ross Snyder, of the Federated Theological Faculty of the University of Chicago, and as here given represents modifications by a class in religious education at Andover Newton Theological School. It may be used in part or as a whole to evaluate a discussion with your neighbors. It should be said, parenthetically, that groups other than neighborhood groups can use the report. A few suggestions will serve to insure its effectiveness.

1. The report should be used with a group that are well established and accustomed to discussing important problems.

2. The report lends itself more to the organized group than to the leaderless or highly informal group discussion. Therefore, it is well to use it on an evening when your neighborhood group are perhaps departing from their usual custom of just talking — when they are seeking, more or less systematically, to arrive at a solution to some problem.

3. It is suitable for an evening set aside for dealing with a neighborhood or community problem that has aroused your group to engage in careful exploration of the issue.

4. Before the discussion starts, each person should understand

that he will have a copy of the report to fill out in order to examine the effectiveness of the group's relations.

5. The report may be found to be an instrument both for increasing the satisfaction of individuals with the group and for improving the group experience.

6. After the discussion, a committee on summary of the report can be chosen to present findings either at the end of the meeting or at the next one. The group should decide, after reading through the report form, whether names will be signed or not.

GROUPNESS REPORT

Name_____ Date_____

Subject of organized
   group discussion_____

INDIVIDUAL LEVEL OF SATISFACTION

1. (*a*) How did you feel this meeting was today?
   _____Failure   _____Poor   _____Fair   _____Good
   _____Very good
  (*b*) Explain why.

A. GROUP SENSE OF DIRECTION

2. To what extent was there a *group sense of direction?* focus? Did the group know what they were trying to do?
   _____Lacking   _____Somewhat vague and confused
   _____Enough to function   _____Good sense of direction
   _____Very good

3. What do you think the group were trying to accomplish today?

4. To what extent were you personally involved?
   _____Meant nothing to me
   _____Felt involved for sake of group
   _____Discussion seemed to come into some of my experience and problem areas
   _____Felt *personally* touched, but kept it to myself
   _____Felt degree of my past, present, future awakened and at stake

5. (*a*) What did you hope to get out of this meeting?

(*b*) To what extent were the things that you personally hoped to get out of the meeting different from what actually happened?

_____Completely opposed   _____Somewhat opposed
_____Unrelated but compatible   _____Fairly similar
_____Identical

B. Group Climate

6. To what extent was there good working atmosphere? people felt free to make their contribution?

_____Oppressive; people afraid to contribute honestly
_____Demanding " Say something "
_____So unstructured not sure contribution wanted, or how to contribute
_____Free to contribute, but much self-consciousness awakened
_____Stimulating, permissive, objective

C. " All Together Within a Common Situation "

7. Sense of depending on each other . . . needed each other for the task and for fellowship. Everyone felt awakened into decision and activity . . . felt others depended upon his decision and activity.

_____It was the leader; we could be passive and spectators
_____Felt need of individual's co-operating with leader
_____Felt assured that a few would carry the ball; rest could keep hidden
_____Felt my personal responsibility, but little need of drawing in other members
_____High degree of interdependence among all members

8. Identification with each other. At home with and trust each other. Each can enter into experiences of others . . . have similar attitudes, needs, experiences.

_____These people are quite different
_____Within the group, there are clusters of people who can understand and work with each other
_____There is enough commonality in our desires and

backgrounds so that we can work together

_____We're pretty much all the same

_____Each is distinctive, but others' important goals and experiences will enrich mine; we feel " at home " with each other

9. What did you feel was the *size* of the group that was interacting most of the time?

    _____Leader in a social vacuum

    _____One person with the leader

  *_____Interaction was only among those who held minority opinions

  *_____Three or four persons in interacting group; rest somewhat passively going along

    _____We, as a single group

*(Note for interpreter of report: All may answer these questions. However, they have more reliability for groups of eight or more.)

D. COMMUNICATION WAS TAKING PLACE

10. To what extent were we contributing honestly our thoughts, experiences, feelings; or just contributing the surface, the trite, being " nice," being and saying what we felt others expected of us?

    _____Marking time

    _____Talking in terms of techniques and methods (no values or personal beliefs)

    _____Saying what we thought our professional role would say; or what we needed to say to fit in with this group

    _____Contributing honestly our feelings, ideas, needs

    _____Really touching off depth concerns — values that we feel strongly about

11. To what extent did others understand your contribution?

    _____Contribution brushed off, disregarded

    _____Contribution rejected, but with an endeavor to understand

    _____Some members responded favorably

    _____The group listened, understood, valued

    _____In addition, the contribution was worked into group creation

12. How much did you endeavor to understand others' contributions?

    _____Felt others should be subordinated to me

    _____Defensive: busy figuring out how to defend my ideas

    _____Somewhat impervious: wrapped up in my own thoughts and feelings

    _____Honestly endeavored to understand others' contributions

    _____Regarded each contribution as coming from the group, and attempted to integrate it into group product

13. (a) How successful were we in integrating different members' ideas and needs into common group ideas and methods?

    _____Failure   _____Poor   _____Fair   _____Good
    _____Very good

    (b) Why?

    _____Unsuccessful: no common product

    _____Each person had possession of goals, ideas, and methods that were compatible but not integrated

    _____Ideas and needs acceptable to the leaders were integrated

    _____Even different ideas and needs were integrated into an underlying group ideology and tradition: boundaries of activity and time were established by the group and accepted by its members

    _____Ideas and needs acceptable to the majority were integrated

E. PRODUCTIVITY

14. Did you find yourself wanting to say things during the meeting that you didn't actually say?

    _____Never   _____A few times   _____Fairly often
    _____Frequently   _____Very often

15. (a) Name key participants who seemed to make the *most valuable* contribution to this discussion.

    (b) What attempts were made to draw others into active participation in the discussion?

16. To what extent was there group creativeness, i.e., " Together we build "?

_____Pretty much one person's ideas

_____Each contribution stood alone

_____A contribution started a " chain reaction." The ultimate product was different

_____A group idea and method were emerging

F. Person to Person Strategies

17. What strategies did you feel that the group members predominantly employed toward you?

_____Toward me, and I was drawn into the group

_____Toward me, but I was not drawn into the group

_____No positive movement

_____Disagreeing, but keeping me in the group

_____Moving against; a threat to me

18. What strategies did you predominantly employ toward others?

_____Moving toward and with them, and drawn into interchange as equals

_____Moving toward and with in order to gain acceptance of others

_____No particular movement to relate myself to anybody

_____Moving away from, rejecting

_____Moving against

G. Happenings to the Self-concept

19. What were the predominant feelings toward self?

_____Felt unfriendly toward myself, critical

_____Feelings unchanged; indifferent

_____Felt friendly toward self

20. Predominant strategies of self.

_____Defensive . . . activity to protect self. Status and prestige defended

_____Complete indifference

_____Outgoing . . . attack on problem at hand . . . self-forgetfully participating in group process

_____See need for change in own methods and personal
attitude . . . and accept it

21. Self-concept of group.
_____We can get along together: choose, decide, plan,
create together
_____We could do better apart from the group
(*a*) _____The group never arrives at any definite
conclusions
(*b*) _____The group does not confine discussions
to the subject
(*c*) _____Other reasons:_____

SUMMARY RATINGS

A. Group's goal awareness; sense of direction
Failure_____   Poor_____   Fair_____   Good_____
Very good_____

B. Group climate
Failure_____   Poor_____   Fair_____   Good_____
Very good_____

C. Sense of groupness
Failure_____   Poor_____   Fair_____   Good_____
Very good_____

D. Communication taking place
Failure_____   Poor_____   Fair_____   Good_____
Very good_____

E. Productivity
Failure_____   Poor_____   Fair_____   Good_____
Very good_____

F. Person-to-person strategies
Failure_____   Poor_____   Fair_____   Good_____
Very good_____

G. Happenings to self-concept
Failure_____   Poor_____   Fair_____   Good_____
Very good_____

Let us suppose that your group — the neighbors — are
about to discuss the question, Shall we permit a Jewish family
to buy a house in our neighborhood? Nine couples have

gathered in Ralph Harris' home. Ralph happens to be the
man from whom most of you bought homes in the new residential section where a dozen families have lived for a period
of four to six years. Sale of houses has lagged, and for a year
now Ralph has had money tied up in a new ranch-type house
that costs more than most people can afford. A few days ago,
after the neighborhood group had enjoyed an evening of discussing trends in education, Ralph placed his problem before
all of you. You were washing dishes in Nell Smith's kitchen
at the time and the crowd knew that Tom Smith would fight
the issue all night unless everyone agreed to postpone discussion until the next meeting. It was decided that Ted Jones, a
good group discussion leader, would be in the chair. That, in
your opinion, would insure thorough and fair expression of
all sides of the problem. You hoped all week that Mary and
Ned West would be present. They could always be counted
on to work hard to expand the group's mind to include a
full hearing of fair employment practices and civil liberties.
But unfortunately Ned had to attend a meeting of the high
school faculty tonight. With Mary present, however, you
know that your position will be strengthened.

Ted puts the question, not forgetting to praise Ralph for
his willingness to follow the custom of the neighbors to bring
a neighborhood problem up for common solution. Ralph reminds Ted that the Jewish question may test the good will
even of their group. You follow the comments back and
forth, noting that Ted keeps the discussion moving directly
on the topic, yet encourages everyone to use plenty of time
to express himself.

You suddenly realize that several of your friends have a
deep, almost bitter feeling against Jews. You say little, for
Mary West is expressing well the point that unless democracy is practiced in favored suburban communities, by groups

of neighbors who respect each other and rely on the fundamental truth that men were meant to have equal rights and
opportunities, then our idealism is sham and our practices
poisonous to society. Mary is pressing Tom Smith pretty
hard. Just how hard you learn as you see that some of Tom's
aversion for Jews is being directed against Mary. Tom is
chairman of the school board, and if he turns against Mary
West, he may make things uncomfortable for Ned West,
who teaches political science at the high school. Tom and
Ned have been known to disagree more than once in the
group, but always their courtesy toward each other has
seemed to mean that they are warm friends. But now you
begin to wonder about their attitudes toward each other, as
Tom takes occasion to remark that some of the ideas Mary
is expressing are the very reason why he is going to insist that
the school board look into the kind of social philosophy that
is being taught their children.

Mary bites her lip, but she is too stirred up to withhold the
thrust that people who gang up to keep Jews out of their
neighborhood are following a Nazi practice.

As Ted brings the discussion back to the central question,
it is plain to you that people have begun to speak with more
caution. You even find yourself believing that fear, an emo-
tion alien to the group's experience up to now, has entered
the room. Viewpoints are being expressed that hardly represent the real beliefs of your friends. With rare skill Ted
works around to a less emotional aspect of the problem and
asks Ralph why he wants to sell the ranch house anyway.
Why not give it to the neighbors for a clubhouse? Ralph's
customary hearty laughter eases the tension, and presently
the group are able to move on with the discussion. An hour
later Ted puts your suggestion to the group that final decision about the sale of the house be postponed until the entire

neighborhood can find a free evening for fuller discussion. Everyone agrees, and Tom has himself sufficiently in check to comment that whatever the decision is to be, he is sure that he and Mary will be able to rely on the judgment of the group. Mary quickly agrees with Tom and so the matter stands.

Ted calls on you to distribute the groupness report forms. Later that night, as you and Ted and Sue Hill, the president of the League of Women Voters, are checking the forms and preparing a summary for the next meeting, you learn some things about how persons operate within a group. You tell yourself, and doubtless you are partly right, that the topic of the evening, being so controversial, accounts for the surprising number of people who have indicated that they were afraid to contribute honestly. Instead of a completely unified group of people, as you had always imagined and as so many of you have often claimed, you find disunity, as evidenced by the fact that about half gave more thought during the discussion either to figuring out how to defend their ideas or to wrapping themselves in their own thoughts and feelings than they gave to an endeavor to understand viewpoints opposed to their own. You are troubled by the failure of the neighbors to integrate their ideas about the Jewish question. According to the report, section G, " Happenings to the Self-concept," few people had a happy evening. But you are encouraged by Ted's comment — based on his reading of the reports — that most of those present still think that they can get along together, can " choose, decide, plan, create together." To which Sue Hill replies that only the stability of the group enables its individuals to have so much faith in each other when deep emotional conflict is aroused.

During the days that follow you reflect long and hard about the meaning of group fellowship, about personal security, about society's dependence upon groupness and how tenuous it is when confronted by partisanship that divides persons into competing and often bitter camps. Yet you know that Sue Hill is right when she sees strength enough in well-established groups to handle controversial problems. Indeed, there is a refining process that comes from fighting through problems which draws persons more compactly together as they learn that mutuality is more precious and personal growth more to be desired than winning a point in favor of some particular bias. The strength and health of a group can be appreciably detected by use of the groupness report, for it abounds in clues that lead to making persons psychologically secure.

III

The following observations about the significance of the report are not numbered to correspond to the items in the report, but they include most of the items and serve as an analysis of the group experience.

1. The individual's level of satisfaction with a particular meeting, or even with a series of discussions, may be rated poor and yet not alienate him from the group — if, over the long run, satisfaction is achieved. The chances are that a person — when consistently dissatisfied — will not remain with a group long enough to register habitual dissatisfaction with what takes place in group sessions. Moreover, it is to be expected that a certain amount of dissatisfaction with discussions serves to draw an individual out, so that he works more closely with the group to give them redirection which not only he as the objector but the group as a whole can find more productive of satisfaction.

2. If most people indicate that they are vague as to the direction in which a group are trying to move, the leadership is faulty and the more alert members are falling down on their usual function: that of helping the leader to bring the group's needs and problems into focus.

3. When persons are truly a group, what they undertake to-gether, far more times than not, will involve most individuals rather deeply. There are times when individuals will check the item in the report that shows they are involved only for the sake of the group. But real groupness means that what goes on in the group touches individuals personally.

4. If the majority of group members constantly get from meet-ings just about what they hoped to get, there is too little develop-ment of persons and too little growth is taking place on the part of the group as a whole. There ought to be considerable achieve-ment by individuals of ideas and understanding unanticipated before the actual group meeting occurs.

5. The psychological climate in which a group meet is not a proper one when mere encouragement is given to speak. Despite freedom to express yourself, you may feel much self-consciousness. The climate produced by stimulating leadership — kindly, evoca-tive, encouraging — and by mutual confidence among the mem-bers provides a permissive atmosphere which is needed for full exchange of thought and planning. In such an atmosphere per-sons are made socially and emotionally secure.

6. The idea behind the phrase, " All together within a common situation " (section C of the report), comes from the responsibility each must feel for all if he is to know the meaning of groupness, of democracy, of fellowship, and of ethical religion. In group dis-cussions some people can and do escape responsibility, riding on the backs of dependable and energetic fellow members. Careful study of point 7, section C, will show to what extent individuals do not share the group load. It may also show where the weakness of the group lies.

7. The unity of your group, or their division into groups within the group, becomes clear as you examine point 8 in the report.

8. Section D, dealing with communication within the group, is especially rewarding to those who seek to know whether or not their fellow group members regard themselves as successful in communicating their thought and feeling. Of all groups the neighborhood group, next to the family, ought to be able to avoid insincere expression, talking to suit some professional role, speaking so as not to disappoint " my public."

9. Unless a group reach a common understanding out of which a common product emerges, discouragement or actual failure will follow. The experience of the neighbors, as cited above, in deciding to postpone decision, to delay the solution to their Jewish problem, was not failure to agree; it was, as a matter of fact, a decision reached in common, held in common, designed to lead to a later and final "common product." A group meeting in which discussion is structured toward problem-solving should never end abruptly, leaving people confused. Agreeing to disagree is better than no clear-cut, vividly stated conclusion to a group discussion.

10. Section E, "Productivity," like all other sections of the report, focuses attention on the creativity of the whole group, on the activity and development of the individual, and on the effectiveness of the leader. If the reports as filled out show much individual productivity that leads to group expression, your group are healthy. The dynamic quality of the true group should stand out clearly under this section and hence indicate the value of the group to the individual members.

11. Under "Person to Person Strategies" (F) an individual is able to see himself more clearly than usual. How you feel toward what you think the predominant thought of the group is doing to you, and how you react to persons, is a self-portrait that can emerge from this section of the report.

12. It is important that each person shall have a friendly regard for himself after his performance in his group. "I could kick myself for saying that," may be due penitence on occasion, but if repeated too often it can destroy the self-esteem essential to healthy relations with persons and essential to inner security. More important than verbal expression is one's unexpressed feeling, which may range all the way from uncritical approval to hostility, neither of which extremes facilitates personal growth or group effectiveness.

IV

The highest quality that can issue from the group experience is that of corporate worship in which the individual experiences the reality of spiritual security.

There are always two reference points in the experience of corporate worship: one is persons; the other is Person. Due regard for the members of the group with whom we are in communion attunes us to that high moment in group relations well known to the Quakers, who rely for decision-making upon the " sense of the meeting."

Let us suppose that a problem has arisen in your neighborhood. Your children, along with others, are not only excluding from their play the children of an Oriental family but also have been smearing paint on the sidewalk in front of their home; now and then they have destroyed property of this Oriental family. You and your marriage partner, together with one or two other couples, have been trying for some time to get your group of neighbors to include the Orientals in your monthly gatherings in the different homes. And tonight the neighbors meet — though without the Oriental couple — and wrestle with what has been taking place among the children.

As usual, the group provide ample opportunity for everyone to express his opinions. During the evening there are some sharp exchanges; for example: " Those people ought to take the hint and move out "; against: " If we can't practice democracy and brotherhood here at home, among the people we can see and learn to know personally, we might as well resign ourselves to the fact that we are all hypocrites! " But the group pass over this encounter without destroying friendships, and presently you are together trying to look honestly at the reasons behind the behavior of your children. Someone tells of an incident that took place among a group of high school young people in a local church. The young people had been discussing what is meant by living the Christian religion, and general agreement had just been voiced calling for inclusion within the church fellowship group of youth of other races. Then it was that a very frank and clear-headed boy said: "I wish I could go along with you on this decision. I know it's right, but my dad would never stand for it."

A silence follows the reporting of this incident. Finally comes the question of a troubled neighbor: "You mean that my kids mistreat the Orientals because they hear me sound off on the subject?"

No one answers, for everyone knows that is about the way things are in Dick's family. At length Dick's wife tentatively comes to his defense: "But, dear, you don't — that is, I'm sure our children have never heard you say they ought to make things miserable for the Orientals."

"No. Of course I've never handed out a set of instructions on how to paint the sidewalk, or how to pull up flowers after dark. But I'll have to confess that my real feelings show through. The fact is, I'm about like a lot of other people. It's easy to see the point of brotherhood, but not so easy to overcome the feelings I've carried around all these years. To be honest, I just can't seem to trust people who are brought up differently, whose religion may be different, and whose eating habits, business methods, and all the rest perhaps run counter to my own."

"But I'm a Methodist and you're a Baptist," someone puts in, to which rejoinder is made that denominational differences within Protestantism are hardly to be compared to Hindu-Christian differences, or to ethnic differences.

Dick's confession leads to similar expression from others present. The very process of sharing individual weaknesses, plus the custom of the neighborhood group of practicing nondefensive exchange of views, leads the group to a higher level on which they are ready to voice the sense of the meeting. Contrary to general procedure, no vote is taken in this group. There is no dividing of one faction over against another. Instead, sincere and respectful efforts are made by the neighbors to understand and work with, rather than against, the thinking and feeling of each other. Thus individuals discover each other, and each person comes close to discovering himself. The man whose inner convictions and feelings may have been understood better by others than by himself is now able to see himself as his neighbors and his family see him. Moreover, he probably finds that others in the group have views close to his own. And yet, because they are striving to reach a higher standard of belief and conduct with regard to the Orientals, he too feels drawn to this higher standard. More than this, because of the sympathetic attitude of his fellows toward him, he is not thrown on the defensive. Rather, his energies are left intact so that he can now use them for his personal growth instead of dissipating them in conflict with his more ethical and emotionally free neighbors.

It is in this sort of permissive atmosphere that a person is accepted, without condemnation, for what he is and for what he may in time come to be. The opponent of all that is Oriental is free to think about his views and to perceive what is required of him if he would change them. He is free because his group do not stir up his emotions, thereby inciting him to defend his views. And because he is clearheaded he can freely choose to go along with the sense of the group, to the end that the Oriental couple will be invited to the next neighborhood evening, at which time games, a singsong, and refreshments are to be enjoyed. (It is significant that the group are wise enough to avoid any head-on discussion of the conflict among the children and are resolved, instead, to rely upon the example of the elders to overcome the present conduct of their children.)

So it is that those of the neighbors who know little about the Oriental couple will have opportunity for themselves to find out what others of the group claim to be the quality of these people: " They're just people, like ourselves; only, maybe a little lonelier."

Very little is said during the evening about Christian idealism, but from the faces of the neighbors it would appear that many thoughts are running through the minds of these friends:

"Respect for personality means *all* personalities — especially those right here in our neighborhood."

"Maybe it is time for us to quit telling our children the story of the Good Samaritan, and to start living it here at home."

"We have prided ourselves on all this neighborliness around here, but all along we have merely enjoyed a mutual admiration society."

"If Dick can admit his real feelings toward the Orientals, and still go along with us in inviting them to our next party, all honor to him."

"Right now, for the first time in a mighty long while, I love these people. They're my neighbors! "

"What a lot of genuine respect the people in this room have for each other. We are close to prayer."

Out of this group experience, wherein persons reach above their biases and narrow concerns to embrace the larger vision of their fellows, worship emerges as a refining quality to elevate and to purify human relations. Such an experience makes ready the entrance of the Spirit of God, to encounter and commune with human spirits. From conflict over a vital community problem, a forthright facing of the problem, and a courageous working through to a solution, men and women are enabled to grow into readiness for worship of the divine Person. Now the individuals and the group as a whole may enter upon the experience of valid worship.

It is undoubtedly true that in private worship a meeting with God is so full of meaning for the worshiper that he relinquishes his will in order to do the will of God. But perhaps only a few people can experience significant private worship; and certainly all persons need rich corporate worship, so that private worship can be sustained and strengthened. As the individual genuinely experiences group worship — in which he chooses to drop his willfulness, in order to abide by the will of the group — he finds that he is prepared to will to do God's will in private, as well as in public. Among his neighbors Dick could choose to adopt the will of his group. For the sake of the neighbors and his children, for the good of all, he felt impelled to resign his will against Orientals and participate in the group's will-to-good toward them.

And Dick's capacity to change bespeaks that of most persons. " For Christ's sake " is, among professing Christians in large numbers as well as among secularists, no longer so much a correct and reverent expression of man's attitude toward divinity as it is a cheap phrase of irreverence. " Love your neighbors for God's sake " carries no imperative, nor even any true and deep meaning to most moderns. But fellowship among neighbors, along the lines recounted above, may indeed convey vital meaning to men who are appealed to, as was Dick, to accept the outcast and make of him a neighbor for the group's sake.

But more than mere acceptance can follow. Men like Dick can learn to value and perhaps to love the outcast. As a part of the group Dick and his kind can, once the venture is made, actually *experience* the meaning of universal brotherhood, by practicing brotherliness in their neighborhoods. And this living out of the ideal of brotherhood brings to life the dry bones of routine worship. The act of communing with persons thus becomes the very process of worship, a process in which individuals make manifest their adoration for God through love of their fellows.

Worship has to become a persistent attitude that enlivens and illumines persons individually and in groups, wherever they are, in whatever circumstances. Precisely in the midst of neighborhood conflicts people must express forbearance, gentleness, sacrifice, devotion, and love that spring from expenditure of friendliness and hope and trust. Persons need to venture, in company with their fellows, into the relatively uncharted area of human brotherhood under the guidance both of a group of friends and of the Father of all men. If institutional religion, through its forms of public worship, seldom evokes the vital experience of learning to value social outcasts, or the experience of communing in spirit and in truth with the God of the universe, then there is all the more reason that men may well tap the resources of a group of their neighbors as a means for enjoying the meaning of worship.

Not all neighborhood experiences, among persons with whom we share life and engage in improving human relations, guarantee that we shall enter into the presence of God. But as we resolve to fashion a way of life in our neighborhood aimed at respecting persons, and doing so with the implicit motive of confronting and honoring God through act more than by word of mouth, we may well be awed over how readily we advance into the presence of the Holy One, the Person of God.

We have often been reminded that worship is no mere matter of training; rather, to experience worship we must establish, confront, and successfully deal with the conditions in which it takes place. These conditions call for our setting right human relations as we encounter the need to do so. We cannot honor God by dishonoring our fellows. And if we would foster group-mindedness and growth of persons in our neighborhoods, then and only then would we value and love them enough to worship God.

From this worship, as the highest achievement of the group process, neighborliness speaks with the voice of love, and enduring fellowship is found by the individual.

3

THE FAMILY: WHERE SECURITY BEGINS

❦   ❦

WITHIN the family we register most sensitively whether or not we are secure; and if we are, the family group are the first to enable us to evidence in our lives that we have the ability to express love, and therefore to enjoy emotional stability. What of the American family today?

In his book *The Family of Tomorrow: The Cultural Crisis and the Way Out,* Carle C. Zimmerman is preoccupied with the plight of the family. He is alarmed not only because of a long-term steadily rising divorce rate in America, but also because the current human behavior is like that which preceded the disintegration of the Roman Empire. Like other students of the family, Zimmerman believes that the recent increase in births is only temporary, and that the popular one- and two-child family will not reproduce enough children to preserve the culture.

Professor Zimmerman examines history and concludes that the family exists to transmit, preserve, and enlarge the culture. He sees great changes occurring " in periods of violent antagonism of the family." Whenever family life has disintegrated, cultural conditions have undergone marked changes. Greece in the third century before Christ, first century Rome, fourth century Rome, Western Europe in the tenth century, all Europe of the fourteenth through the sixteenth centuries, eighteenth century France, nineteenth century Russia, and the Western culture in this century constitute the times of "uncoupling of the family from the culture." In these periods the restraints exercised by family mores are cast off and cultural patterns undergo decisive breakup and reorganization. Today, as in fourth century Rome, sex is man's master and the family is in decline.

This persuasive sociohistoric inquiry insists that rejection of familism means rejection of culture. What Burgess and Locke call individualism (*The Family: From Institution to Companionship*), Zimmerman refers to as atomism; both bespeak the opposite condition to familism, in which the welfare of the family group is rated ahead of the desires of the individual. In the fourth century the clan-trustee family emerged to take over as the atomistic family declined and the rising Christian Church sought to institute reforms. Jerome, Augustine, and other Church Fathers brought Christian doctrine to bear on a sociology of the family. Though Jerome fostered asceticism, encouraged monasticism, and seemed to discount the family, he was against divorce. Augustine, a convert from Manichaeanism — which approved sexual relations but not the birth of children — favored family stability. And while the world entered into centuries of darkness, the Church Fathers — who were not " cultural determinists " but leaders who met the challenge of the times for establishing fresh directions — pointed to a higher world. It was the City of God against the City of Earth.

Religious leaders provided cultural redirection. Now, as then, cultural renewal requires re-creation of the family as a unit that is regarded as being very nearly sacramental. While Professor Zimmerman makes no plea that church leaders rally for the salvation of the family and thus achieve the preservation of Western culture, he does draw heavily upon the thought of ancient spiritual leaders. In his view the family is not only a private affair but it is also social and contains a value " more fundamental in importance than sex, companionship, individual willfulness, or any other social, economic, or biological aim " (p. 233).

Twenty-one students of the family contributed to the volume *The Family: Its Function and Destiny,* edited by Ruth Nanda Anshen. This book contains both knowledge and wisdom which if used might go far toward assuring enlightened regard for the family as a source and vehicle of culture. For the most part, the authors succeed in imparting their confidence that the destiny of the family and society is something less dire than present evidence portends. Ruth Benedict insists that " the anthropologist knows that the changes taking place in the home in any decade in any country do not mean that the family is now about to disintegrate . . . unless we do something about it " (p. 159). In America, at least, the family has become democratic. It has withstood difficult times. True, it may be that the family is " moving with precipitous speed to greater and greater atomization and destruction " (Miss Anshen). Authoritarianism in the political realm is induced by the home situation in which the father " is replaced by collective entities " (Max Horkheimer), with the school athletic team, the club, the state assuming his prerogatives. Confronted by a crisis in loyalties, the secularization of life, and continued competition between religion and science (A. L. Swift, Jr.), we can but conclude that family life, like society as a whole, endures troubled times.

This is a symposium and therefore it is not required to present a single, neat view. It would seem that its purpose has been achieved " to refute the pragmatic, naturalistic, and empirical theory of the family as . . . propounded by . . . Westermarck, Marx, Engels " (p. 4).

What is the destiny of the family? This may not present fairly the composite view of the authors (if indeed there is one), but it will not be far amiss to say that they expect *some kind of family life* to endure. Rapid changes now taking place must be considered philosophically. Moral values embedded within the structure of man's long history (his social development), within the family itself, and within religion permit no mere biological interpretation of human behavior and no succumbing to pure Freudianism.

But individual desires and whims are replacing a sense of responsibility to the family. Our society is suffering from considerable family disintegration, caused not alone by broken homes but also by loss of felicity and love within families where no divorce or desertion has occurred. Excessive individualism and widespread tensions attest to this loss of primary group solidarity. Social workers, guidance experts, psychiatrists, and personnel officers in many fields recognize that, as an isolate, a person cannot be adequately helped. He and his family have to be dealt with. Today we are confronted by the need to furnish redirection both for the family and for Western society. The destiny of each is linked with the other. When a family succeeds in transmuting its life into a spiritual relationship, it is engaging in stabilizing human society. And the relationship among the members of the family must be one of fellowship, in which its members value each other highly, expressing mutual regard, appreciation, concern, and selflessness.

I

In the family, as in other primary groups, fellowship is established when individuals conduct themselves in terms of the worth they recognize in each other. This means that mutuality and sharing govern parent-child relations and parent-parent relations, unless parents retard or destroy family fellowship either through ignorance or through feelings of hostility. Because much of contemporary life fosters individualism instead of familism, an adult or child often develops hostility toward persons within the family whose interests and needs vie with his desire to go his way unimpeded. Individualism really means that a parent does not want to be a parent. Resentment due to the inescapable fact that he is a parent breaks out in antagonistic conduct toward the other parent and toward the children who have trapped him in the confines of parenthood. Dissensions follow and family well-being is undermined as escape is sought in time spent away from the home and its parental responsibilities. The father may work longer hours than necessary at the office while shopping tours of undue length, numerous civic activities, poor housekeeping, and the like typify the mother's rejection of the family. And when demands of the family are not placed ahead of the individual's desires, family unity is canceled and the first step — which may prove decisive — has been taken toward disintegration of the home.

Psychiatrists can sometimes help parents to gain perspective on their true condition, enabling them to understand their real attitudes. But restoration or salvation of the person for worthy parenthood is basically a spiritual and religious task. In the family, more than in any other group, religious behavior and devotions are required for achieving fellowship. This achievement comes by means of continuing experiences in which adults succeed in teaching children by example to be consistently respectful to one another and to their parents, co-operatively and enthusiastically and adventurously finding a common way with parents through difficulties — and having fun in doing so.

Jackie asks, "Why?" seventy-nine times a day. Why do birds eat worms? Why does the rain wet the ground? Why do trees and flowers need water? Why can't Mother take him to the store again today? Mother may think every "why" is aimed at annoying her. This is not the case unless her manner has invited annoyance, or unless she has shown Jackie that she has no time, interest, or imagination with which to help him to find answers to his first "why." Children's questions and parents' attitudes provide the materials for making family relations productive of fellowship, educational growth, and emotional and spiritual health. But adults must handle these materials wisely, remembering that family patterns are established when the children are young. If preschool children do not find rapport with parents, this failure will cause them, during adolescence, to become problems to themselves, to their parents, and possibly to society. Security begins, if at all, in the home.

Before the first child is weaned, his parents ought to begin drawing up their own policy for making family life an educational and religious venture. Neither policy nor parental conduct can wait, for by the time the child is a few months old he begins to pattern his behavior according to that of his parents, as evidenced by his ability to mimic a parent's facial expression. If he could talk, his tone of voice would be like that of his parents. And if he were able to express himself as do adults, he would use the style of expression used by his parents, for he is very early able to absorb the mood, conduct, and values of those closest to him.

A set of working principles for young parents who intend to nurture secure children might begin with the following:

1. Because we want our child to respect us, we must regularly speak respectfully to each other in his presence, starting when he is a baby.

2. Because we desire him as a child and man to meet each situation and problem patiently and reasonably, we should be unhurried, calm, and rational when preparing and giving him his bottle, cleaning up after him, dressing him, and guiding his first play.

3. We need to respect the child's own rate of growth, neither censuring him because of mistakes nor hurrying his social and physical performance.

4. We must strive for an optimistic outlook on life, qualified by realism.

5. To talk about our child in his presence or to exhibit him as a prize performer before friends is harmful to him and a mark of parental immaturity.

6. We must avoid criticizing others, complaining about disappointment, or being defeatist.

7. Believing as we do that children respond to guidance, we shall need to equip ourselves through reading, study, and observation of others' successful guidance of children.

8. When failure comes, it is to be viewed as an experience helpful in avoiding further failure.

9. Recognizing that parents are of most importance to the successful development of children, we must adopt a consistent course for our labors with our child.

10. Fun together will ease the rough spots.

11. Participation with other parents in suitable groups and organizations can help us to do a better job within the family.

12. In order to answer a child's questions, we shall have to strike a balance between enough and too much talk.

13. Nagging destroys affection and trust, but definite reminders must be given the child at all stages of growth.

14. If we would gain respect and love, we must exercise respect and express love.

15. Parents ought not to do everything, nor too little, for the child; neither make every decision for him nor overload him with responsibility; neither laugh at him nor refrain from laughing with him; neither pose as omniscient nor always mumble, "I don't know"; neither lie to him nor tell lies in his presence; neither take advantage of him nor permit his taking advantage of others.

16. No child is perfect, even as no adult is perfect.

17. No family lives unto itself, separated from other persons and society.

18. The mental health of children is largely in the hands of parents.

19. The spiritual worth of persons is largely determined by the homes from which they come.

20. Accumulated abuse, defeat, and rejection suffered in childhood destroy personality.

21. Accumulated good humor, trust, affection, security, and zestful attacks on ordinary issues of living provide secure, affectionate, and competent persons capable of meeting extraordinary problems of life.

22. Behavior is symptomatic. Misbehavior is symptomatic of the child's difficulty with himself — a difficulty that is generally rooted in a parent's difficulty.

23. Discipline means learning to exercise inner controls — controls that seldom are established merely by external pressure that takes the form of physical punishment.

24. When in doubt, don't bluff; the child is not deceived, but confused and made insecure.

25. When wrong, admit it. When right, don't rub it in; rubbing it in drives either the marriage partner or the child out of your affection.

26. " Let not the sun go down upon your wrath."

27. Marriage is more than companionship of a man and woman; it is a wider relationship which requires, for its nurture, fellowship inclusive of each member of the family.

II

The nursery school offers one of the best ways for parents to get help in training their children and developing secure homes. First, it has to be a good school. *Our Cooperative Nursery School,* the story of the Silver Spring (Maryland) nursery school project, provides a plan which any group of parents could adapt to meet their own needs. This particular program employs expert leadership plus rotation of volunteers, wives and husbands, for performing the many services demanded by a self-supporting school. The best feature of volunteer help is that parents are being educated for their home tasks as they could not be merely by a hit-or-miss process, or through reading of books. All activities of the Maryland program are considered as parent education.

Secondly, the nursery school should open the way for creating secure homes through a counseling program. In the following account it will be noted that the school provides a setting for opening counseling with parents whose child is found by the teacher to need particular help. In many instances, as in this case, the nursery school is not adequate for correcting a given family situation at its source. It is the parent who requires help.

Here is an account of a guidance process initiated by a competent teacher, who stops at the outer limit of her resources and refers parents to a skilled counselor:

The Taners have one child, Gene, aged three and a half. The nursery school teachers find that negativism controls him long after he should have outgrown this stage. Unlike a two-and-a-half- or three-year-old, Gene does not respond to any efforts to divert him, to change his attitude by humor or by playing games with him. During story time and singing he is seldom at ease, either annoying the child beside him or fidgeting so much as to rule out his listening or singing. Gene does not know how to share toys, or to take turns, or to help in cleaning up the room.

As a part of the services of the school to the child, the teachers regularly interview parents; and Miss Oley, the head teacher, realizes that an early discussion with Gene's parents is necessary. By telephone she arranges to see the mother and father together. Unlike many fathers, Mr. Taner is quick to volunteer the information that his failure to handle Gene properly is the cause of the child's maladjustment.

"I can save you a lot of time, Miss Oley," Mr. Taner begins. "My wife agrees that Gene is rebelling because he has had enough of my impatience. I'm a perfectionist, and I know I demand too much of him."

Mrs. Taner: "I do think, Miss Oley, that my husband is beginning to be easier on Gene."

Mr. Taner: "Don't alibi for me, dear. As a matter of fact, I've known for several months that my iron discipline is no good with a child. The trouble is, I take things out on the kid."

The conversation lasts for a full hour, at the conclusion of which Miss Oley knows that Mr. Taner needs more help than she can give. He seems to understand the seriousness of Gene's problem, but neither he nor his wife shows much confidence that he will be able to correct things. So it is that Mr. Taner decides, under Miss Oley's deft handling, that he will seek counsel elsewhere.

But help takes effect slowly, for Mr. Taner has to spend an hour or two a week for more than a year with the psychiatrist to whom he is referred. At the outset he has the notion that his insistence on Gene's always having clean hands, keeping his room tidy, not making any noise around the house, and speaking with adult politeness to neighbors and guests, derives from some forgotten incident of sexual guilt during childhood. But before counseling is terminated with Mr. Taner's readjustment to himself and to Gene, he understands that most of his life as a child was spent in feeling unable to keep up with what his own father expected of him. In summing up, Mr. Taner tells his counselor:

"I always knew that my poor school work and inferior athletic ability disappointed my father. I felt guilty because of failing him, especially since he liked to brag to his friends, even before I got out of rompers, how I was going to outshine all the kids at school. It was an awful blow to him when I failed at college. At examination time I would usually get sick at my stomach and hand in unfinished work. I have never had a good job — one that was white-collar enough to suit my wife. Until the last few weeks nothing could have convinced me that she married me for any reason other than sympathy or pity for me. Now that is cleared up. I know she loves me as I am. Before Gene was born, I vowed to myself that I'd start right out training him to be a world beater. I filled his cradle with toys — rewards, I called them — for not crying, for not spilling his bottle, and so forth. I know I tried to bribe him to learn toilet training too early and made him nervous by shaming him, telling him I would not love him if he wet his pants. When he was learning to walk and would fall down, I complained that he would never be an athlete if he was clumsy. If he rebelled when I tried to poke food in his mouth and pour milk down his throat, I told him he would be a weakling. Now I see that I was unconsciously following my own dad's methods — which practically ruined me."

Mr. Taner not only clarified his situation but effected the change in himself necessary for him to let Gene develop at his own rate. He began by avoiding overattention to the child, though holding himself ready to help to tie a shoelace, mend a toy, button difficult clothes, and the like. He was more sparing in his comments, avoiding blame and praising Gene enough to show him that he is appreciated.

Ordinarily parents are faced only by simple difficulties, which may be recognized at nursery school before they are in the home. Indeed, all that most parents need to understand is that theirs are not the only problems that people have in bringing up children. Ordinarily, too, what most fathers and mothers need is help in getting hold of the right books and pamphlets on child development and encouragement to work with competent nursery teachers so that the child may enjoy consistent treatment in school and home. It is quite true that adults, in as serious trouble as Mr. Taner, usually would not be so willing or so able as he to confess their faults. But the skill of the nursery teacher and the desire of Mr. Taner to do what might be necessary to help his child, plus a wife who actually believed in him and who, as he came to see, really loved him, started him toward recovery which depended finally on good counseling.

It is obvious that the nursery teacher should be not only a child expert; she must also serve as a family guide, a function that requires a mature, poised, and competent woman for dealing with adults. This is a high requirement, and, despite the growth over the country in recent years of nursery education, there are too few workers and too few schools to serve the family as it needs to be served today. Public education may be counted on eventually to make nursery classes a part of the educational system, but until that time community groups, churches, and other institutions will need to provide nursery education.

III

Many parents are at a loss as to how to cope with the problems of family relations and guiding their children toward maturity. In general it seems true that parents who are successful with preschool children have a good chance to be equally successful when the children reach adolescence. If parental success with children does not precede the adolescent period, it is often too late for the family to enjoy fellowship. But some families can begin, though belatedly, to show respect for each person in the group; and all should at least try to discuss allowances, dating, school problems, religious perplexities, social and emotional anxieties that accompany adolescence. It is never too late to attempt the use of democracy within the home, to practice treating the other fellow as a person who has rights and responsibilities and who needs encouragement when he fails, support when he is in trouble, and sympathy when nothing seems to offer him hope.

But family relations are best when developed over the years, as was done in the Smith home. At the dinner table the Smiths are discussing Dad's offer of a new job in a distant city. Betty, fifteen and securely established with her high school crowd, is near tears at the very thought of having to leave town. Tad, eighteen, has only six months to go to graduate with his class, of which he is an officer and a key figure. Mrs. Smith does not want to leave the community where she and the family have lived happily for fifteen years, but on the other hand she knows that her husband has been given a rare opportunity to render wider service and she is, as always, ready to undertake with him whatever seems best. Mr. Smith is reluctant to uproot his family, and at his age he is not keenly desirous of venturing on a new job. Besides, he thinks he is serving God and man where he now is.

Betty has to hurry off to an evening rehearsal of the girls' glee club, Tad has a date, and so the Smiths decide to devote an evening later in the week to analyzing the pros and cons of the new offer.

Meantime an insistent letter comes to Mr. Smith and he begins to feel that he ought to make the move. Mrs. Smith remains as she was, loath to go but ready to advance her husband's career. Both Tad and Betty have decided to play for time, hoping that they do not have to move at least until summer and preferably not at all.

The discussion reopens in the living room on Saturday evening after all four members of the family have done the dishes. Mother has been cautioning them not to mix serious discussion with drying the chinaware; Dad has been teasing

Betty about the six dates she has broken in order to remain home for the evening.

The family enumerate all the reasons why they should move and all the feelings each person has that make moving objectionable. At length they reach an impasse, until Mother reminds them that their final decision about this problem, as always, must be in accordance with what they believe to be the mission of the Smith family. And because the family has through the years been drawn together to make corporate decisions, rather than individual decisions, because it is a unity in fellowship, each member is able to make a decision based on principles and devotions higher than personal desire.

And so the Smiths decide to move. Betty does not abandon herself to tears, for Mother taught her as a child of five how to face reality. When her tonsils had to be removed, Mother had told her the Martin and Judy stories about sickness and hospitals (Volume 2), which prepared her for the pain and avoided the fear that many children suffer when they are deceived about illness. Tad is to be left behind in order to graduate with his class, but he is ready to look after himself, to conduct himself responsibly while he lives apart from the family. When he was a child, his parents had let him help with household chores, not scolding him when he broke a dish and praising him when he learned to handle delicate objects with care. Neither parent had done for him what he could do for himself. Both children always got simple, clear answers to whatever questions they asked. If at first Mother and Dad did not know the answers, they could be depended on to set out on a venture with the children to find the answers.

To be sure, there had been defaults from this high stand-

ard. Once Dad discovered that some of " the funnies " Tad
was reading contained a lot of nonsense about the sanctity of
the economic *status quo*. Also he found that most of the funnies were filled with nightmarish spectacles suitable only for
ruining a small boy's peaceful sleep. " Absolutely no more of
that stuff in this house! " he declared. It took a long time for
Mother to show him that that fiat would destroy the children's confidence in their parents, besides driving the funnies — and Tad — underground.

There had been another and worse problem, from Mother's point of view, when a distant relative came for a visit,
bringing along his bias against " foreigners." Because the
children loved " Uncle," as did their parents, it was particularly difficult to set up antibodies against this subtle infection.
The Smiths were hardly prepared to deal with such a car-
rier of prejudice and soon Tad was heard telling Uncle that
he guessed he would never play on a team with a bunch of
" Wops " and " Dagos." Betty, then six years old, informed
one of her most beloved playmates — a charming Jewish
child of a German refugee family — that she would never,
never in this world play with " those lousy foreigners " because her uncle had said they were all dirty and ought to be
sent back where they came from. Both parents found themselves issuing orders about what children are to believe and
not believe, declaring that such rot ill becomes any decent
family's attitudes. Even before their guest left, Mother went
so far as to add to the children's distress by telling them that
Uncle would never again darken their door. It took a lot of
restudy and diligence for the Smiths to get back on even
keel.

Together Mother and Dad had succeeded in counteracting
the funnies and Uncle's ideas. Either Mother or Dad regularly read the comics and discussed the stories with Tad and

Betty, giving them interpretations more in keeping with the views of their parents. Likewise the family began a project of exploring the history of America, examining together the great experiment of many cultures in one, and entertaining "foreign" children whom Tad and Betty were willing to invite home with them from school.

Mother was to remember these experiences when the children had reached adolescence. Tad was fourteen or fifteen when he began to stay out late after high school parties. Dad lost his poise one evening and began to shout orders that no son of his could prowl around until one and two o'clock Sunday morning. All Tad said was, " I'm no kid." What he did was to stay out late the following Saturday night. Mother was awake when she heard the front door open and slipped downstairs ahead of Dad. During the father-son scene that followed she remained hidden behind the sofa where she had connected the electric recorder. The next afternoon, when the children were away, she played the recording while Mr. Smith's face got redder and redder.

At the end of ten minutes' recording he gasped, " If I had a father who talked like that to me I'd shoot him, or leave home permanently! "

Since Dad had heard himself as others hear him, he had been not only a chastened but a reformed father. " I always thought that it was devastating enough to see ourselves as others see us; now I know a worse fate: to hear myself as Tad had to hear me! "

Because the adult Smiths have always had enough intelligence and good will, cemented by trust and love for each other and the children, Tad and Betty have grown — reversals notwithstanding — into their places as maturing, responsible members of a family group who can talk and think together, reaching decisions together. This fellowship was at work when they agreed that Dad ought to take the new job. It is a relationship that fortifies them for times of triumph and times of disappointment. It has enabled them to depart, on many occasions, from the standards of society that they believe to be faulty or evil. It is a fellowship that can suffer no defeat even when death comes. The Smiths have a quality of life suitable for release throughout a sickened and dissolving society, a quality that can provide persons with spiritual security.

IV

As young men the Jonson brothers liked to think back on their home life. When he went to college, Carl Jonson had occasion to write his autobiography. He recalled his early introduction to books. One day, when he was about three years old, little Carl appeared in his father's study and began to select a number of books within reach. "This is a psychological book," he commented, moving some sort of volume from shelf to table. "And here is a Jesus book," he observed, departing to find his mother so that she could read a story to him before he went to bed.

Carl had heard his parents refer to certain of their books on psychology. He liked the sound of the big word and used it, together with other new words, on frequent occasions. The "Jesus book" was similar to one in the modern series, *My Book,* by Mary Edna Lloyd.

After Carl's little brother Joey was born, Mr. and Mrs. Jonson took turns putting the children to bed. Before the children went to sleep, one and sometimes both parents spent from five to twenty minutes with the boys chatting as fancy directed, listening to their reflections on the day, answering their countless questions, and being silent for brief moments with them. Mrs. Jonson began the custom when she learned that religious educators recommend quiet times of this kind during which preschool children tell what they have enjoyed during the day. The Jonsons soon found that the children would ask questions about things that puzzled or troubled them. This became the time when reassurance was most easily given, and when original prayers or simple verse prayers were used. Sometimes the mother or father would pray, thanking God for a specific happening, appreciated and valued by adult and child alike, asking that each might remember to be more gentle tomorrow, more co-operative and loving. A quiet song might be sung. (Before he was three, Joey would ask Mother to sing " The Lord's Prayer." One night when his turn came to pray, he sang a few measures of the song and finished by speaking accurately all the rest of the words in the prayer.)

Father believed that the times when the children and the parents were genuinely worshipful came when a child, under the stimulus of a story, would ask a question about growth. The questions would lead to recognition that " the wonder part " about persons and other growing things is too deep for explanation. This was in the days before the Martin and Judy stories, but all the Jonsons learned later — through their friends who had younger children — to be grateful to Verna Hills and Sophia L. Fahs for their Martin and Judy books. As baby sitters, the Jonson boys often used the three volumes of stories as well as the songbook. In the living room, around the piano, Carl and Joey would sing while their young charges might just listen, or perhaps clap rhythmically in childish glee. With stories and songs the boys taught the younger children to enjoy, instead of fearing, thunderstorms. (" Hark, Thunder Growls " was especially effective during storms.) The stories taught the children to look forward in spring to planting a garden and to exploring nature, and encouraged them to follow the example of Martin and Judy in helping with simple household chores.

Any member of the Jonson family would say that Jeanette Perkins Brown's collection of singing graces is suitable for a young family to use in worship at mealtime. By the time they were in school, either of the Jonson boys or Father or Mother would select a hymn or lead the family prayer at evening devotions. Mrs. Jonson would tell her friends that prayer and song did as much to develop good eating and bedtime habits as did the counsel available in parents' manuals.

The Jonson boys liked to remember that when their parents read to them, they avoided hurry and used proper enunciation. They read with animation, but were not overdramatic. A. A. Milne's Christopher Robin, in verse and story, became a household favorite. The children liked Robert Louis Stevenson's *Child's Garden of Verses* and soared in imagination with tales by Hans Christian Andersen. When Carl and Joey learned to read, some evenings were spent practicing aloud with their school readers, but all through grammar school and the adventure period of the preadolescent, the parents found time to read with them stories of courage and daring. Sometimes Father would read a psalm with poetic feeling, and now and then one of the children would ask that a favorite passage be read with a musical background provided by Mother at the piano.

With family reading, stories, and music, there naturally went family discussion. Carefully chosen community and world affairs were discussed in the presence of the children who, at eight or nine years of age, began to take a discerning part in reflective conversation. The boys early learned to use ideas and to deal intelligently with social issues.

But it was not only what the family read together, or what

they did together and talked over, that nurtured the boys. The intellectual, artistic, and religious pursuits of each parent, reading or painting or meditating alone, bespoke the values and character of the father and mother. Thinking back on this, Carl included in his autobiography, as a freshman at college:

"The familiar sight of my parents surrounded by books of poetry, philosophy, history, biography, and religion always made me want to get inside those tomes — to hear the music, partake of the ideas, hold intercourse with the minds and lives of the great. I knew, somehow without being told, that what fed the minds of my parents issued in the great-heartedness of their lives, in their vital, low-pitched, calm, and deep conversation together, in their unfailing delight in talking and playing and working with my brother and me. Even when Dad would ask us to mow the lawn, his very tone would herald a pleasant venture. When Mother talked with us about our day at school, her dialogue could be as interesting as a stage play. I do not exaggerate when I say that ideas, not gossip, prevailed in our home because my parents held converse with the world's masters in literature, music, art, and religion.

"In our house we ate well, but Mother knew how to come out of the kitchen and Dad never lost himself behind a newspaper when we boys might benefit from a diet of thinking and living, for which I am profoundly grateful. My parents have never forgotten how to alternate between their own intellectual pursuits and sharing mental and spiritual fellowship with the family."

As our homes fare, so fares the social order. Our society and Western civilization are undergoing drastic change that threatens further individual and social breakdown. This is evidence that family fellowship and stability are limited to relatively few homes today. But within family life there can be a citadel of personal security and social stability such as individuals too seldom experience. And when persons need individual help, they may look to the religious counselor.

4

WORK WITH INDIVIDUALS

❧ ❧

THE SCRIPTURAL injunction that we are to bear one another's burdens relates directly to the psychological fact that people need assistance when the load gets too heavy. Most of us can stand upright when responsibilities are not extraordinary. But when difficulties mount and we seem to have to handle them alone, almost anyone may feel that his foundations of faith and experience are slipping away into insecurity. At that moment there should be no hesitation in finding a counselor with whom to join forces for establishing emotional stability and spiritual security.

For many years the late Dr. Harrison S. Elliott, of Union Theological Seminary, used the phrase "work with individuals" to denote the counseling relationship as it may exist between a practicing psychologist, or a teacher, case worker, or minister, and the individual who seeks him out for help. Counseling on ordinary life problems, as distinguished from that which is done only by a competent analyst or psychiatrist in handling deeper problems, properly falls within the scope of professional service, which some teachers, pastors, and others are capable of giving because of aptitude, training, and experience. But the person who seeks help from any counselor should always be prepared to be referred to some other and more suitable counselor. Likewise the counselor should be ready to indicate to the counselee when he needs to go elsewhere. No counselor and no person in difficulty need feel any reluctance to drop an initial plan to enter into a counseling relationship. Just as a patient is usually willing to leave his doctor, upon the doctor's recommendation, and go to a specialist, so the person who approaches his pastor with a personality problem should be quite ready to be passed on to a psychiatrist if the pastor finds this step desirable or necessary.

Anyone who is troubled by a difficulty found to be in-organic — a functional disturbance not caused by physical illness — is wise to select a counselor known to be trust-worthy and competent. There is no magic in counseling; rather, cause-effect relations are uncovered by means of the combined efforts of the counselor and the counselee, so that the latter may advance his intention to see himself as he is, and frequently understand how he got that way, the better to live in the future more realistically, and hence more happily, productively, and wholesomely.

To the church counseling room in a large city come many people in trouble. The sessions reported below are essentially factual, but certain details have been changed or omitted for the sake of guarding the identity of the people involved. The first case shows that temporary help was given; but it offers little reason to think that this family moved very far toward spiritual maturity. Rather, it illustrates how acutely families like this one need spiritual foundations before their frictions can be overcome.

I

Mr. Ball is at the end of his resources. He says he is willing to do anything to establish harmony in his home. With scarcely a pause he talks for an hour about the bickering between his wife and two adolescent children. He wants the older child — an unmarried mother — and his wife to see the counselor.

Counselor: I shall be glad to see them, if they care to come.

Mr. Ball: Oh, the girl will do what I tell her — what I suggest.

Counselor: She is accustomed to following your advice.

Mr. Ball: Yes, I get along with her. I sort of take care of that with her allowance. And I've been pretty good to her during her trouble.

Counselor: She relies on you.

Mr. Ball: Yes, she is closer to me than to her mother, but her mother has taken her into the home again and nothing is said about the baby. We arranged for its adoption. My daughter may appreciate what her mother has done, but she doesn't show it. As I say, they fight all the time. I can hardly stand to go home at night. The trouble is, the wife tells Jill she can't go out with a certain fellow — a chap she has known for a long time, before even she met the father of the baby.

Counselor: Jill likes the boy she is dating?

Mr. Ball: We don't really know. I guess she is lonely and wants to get married someday. But the trouble is my wife tells her this present boy is no good; doesn't want him in our house. That makes Jill stay out late. We don't know what she's getting herself into with this fellow. My wife nags her all the time. It's enough to drive me crazy.

Counselor: You will ask them to come in for a talk?

Mr. Ball: Nothing would please me more. I think I can get the wife to come too.

Mrs. Ball and Jill came and each was seen separately. Jill was antagonistic from the start. Obviously she had merely complied with her father's wish that she visit the counselor. She slumped into the chair and said nothing.

Counselor: Your father wanted you to come here.

Jill: Yes.

Counselor: You didn't want to come.

Jill: What good will it do?

Counselor: What good will it do?

Jill: Nothing can do me any good. It's her. It's all her fault.

Counselor: Your mother's fault?

Jill: Yes. She's — she's — sometimes I think she is crazy.

The girl spoke vehemently and it was evident that she was extremely hostile toward her mother. Also it was obvious that Jill wanted no help from the counselor. Still, she was at least in the counseling room and, as long as she was there, there remained the possibility that she might profit by the counseling experience.

Counselor: If you had two wishes, what would you wish for most?

Jill (beginning to cry): I want to get married — to be loved; and I want to be trusted.

Counselor: You want your mother to trust you.

Jill: Yes. She never has trusted me. She was always after me, like she was afraid of something.

Jill told the story of her early adolescence. She tried to have both boy and girl friends, but she always found that her mother would insult them when they came to the house. She had learned nothing about sex from her mother, and the little information she had picked up in high school had not helped her. She was able to recognize that her mother had stuck by her, and that Mrs. Ball had endured humiliation in the eyes of the community because her daughter had had an illegitimate child. Furthermore, she was grateful to her father for his attitude toward her. Toward him she manifested something close to love, but for her mother she maintained a combination of hostility and misunderstanding. It was as if she had never known her mother.

Jill came back only once, and this time of her own volition. She remained firm in her conviction that it was her mother who in their household most needed counseling, who most needed to change her way of life. As for herself, was it not enough that she was not going astray again, and that she had resumed attending her church?

Mrs. Ball was rather agitated when she first entered the counseling room. Although the room provides complete privacy and is, in appearance, more like a comfortably furnished living room than an office, her manner bespoke uneasiness and embarrassment. It was evident that though she was somewhat curious as to what might transpire, this factor alone was not strong enough to have brought her for counseling. She was there because of her husband's urging. She started off by telling about her humiliation in the eyes of her friends, whom she had avoided " since Jill's disgrace." She found it difficult to talk about the illegitimate birth, and complained bitterly about Jill's staying out late every night. Plainly Mrs. Ball distrusted both her daughter and the boy whom she was dating.

Counselor: You are wondering what your daughter is doing out late.
Mrs. Ball: Yes, wouldn't you, under the circumstances?
Counselor: You feel she may get into trouble again.
Mrs. Ball: Once a criminal, always a criminal.

Mrs. Ball returned weekly for seven conferences. As time passed, she could examine fairly realistically the factors that led up to Jill's rebellion. Two main facts emerged:

Counselor: What about the early childhood of your children?
Mrs. Ball: Oh, we got along beautifully. I waited on the babies hand and foot. I still do everything for Jill. She does nothing around the house — doesn't even keep her own room clean. And look at her; what good has my slaving for her done?

Counselor: Um-m.

Mrs. Ball: Why couldn't Jill turn out as well as my son? They both had the same advantages, a good home and everything done for them. We've always been church people. I just can't see why this awful thing happened.

Counselor: You loved both of the babies and took good care of them yourself.

Mrs. Ball: I had a maid but I always looked after Jill just as much as I did her brother.

Counselor: Jill is the older child?

Mrs. Ball: Yes.

Counselor: You planned for her? You wanted to have a baby?

But Mrs. Ball had not planned for Jill, did not want her, and had never accepted her. This fact was clearer to the counselor than to the mother. Indeed, Mrs. Ball did not realize that she had rejected her daughter. She was a failure as a mother, for she was still too much fixed on her own unhappy and rejected childhood. Perhaps more extensive counseling would have helped her, had she chosen to continue coming for much longer than she did.

Now for the other fact that emerged:

Counselor: What about your own childhood?

Mrs. Ball: Well, I had a good mother, though she died when I was eleven. Then I went to live with an aunt — an old person — who brought me up. I lived with my aunt and uncle until I married Mr. Ball when I was eighteen.

Counselor: Your aunt was also good to you?

Mrs. Ball: Yes, but I was glad to get away — when I married.

Counselor: About your children: Did you explain sex to them?

Mrs. Ball: No. Why should I? They had courses on that subject in high school.

Counselor: And no one ever explained sex to you, as a child?

Mrs. Ball: No one.

Counselor: You don't like to talk about sex, do you?

Mrs. Ball (a nervous laugh): No, I guess I don't.

During further counseling it became clear that Mrs. Ball had never accepted Jill because she herself had not been accepted as a child, either by her own mother or by her aunt with whom she went to live at the age of eleven and from whose home she was glad to escape into marriage, even though she went as an unprepared bride of eighteen. Mr. Ball indulged both his children and his wife. He sought to keep peace by giving them too much money and too many luxuries. Gradually, during counseling, Mrs. Ball began to see that her nagging and emotional outbursts were no more mature than Jill's behavior. She learned to talk with some ease about her dependence upon her husband, and, in a measure, she sensed that her continued waiting on her children kept them from growing into responsibility and maturity. She did not go far enough with the counseling to gain insight into her reason for being oversolicitous for her household. She probably never grasped the fact that she unconsciously tried to erase her guilt over rejecting Jill by picking up her clothes, cleaning her room, cooking for her, seldom calling on her to wash dishes, and by keeping constant check on her dating.

But Mrs. Ball did make some progress, so she and her husband both reported, toward giving Jill more freedom to see her friends. She worked out with her husband and the counselor a plan whereby Jill was given the opportunity to help with the housework. She restrained herself from handing down rigid rules for her daughter to follow and, to some extent, she became less fearful that Jill might get into trouble again. Admittedly the progress made was not enough for one to say that Mrs. Ball had been re-educated, but she was able to resume her church and community activities and to meet her friends again.

II

Work with individuals supplements group work. There are times when a person with a problem derives greater aid from a group, and times when only the privacy and intensive attention in an individual setting is helpful. Ultimately a person needs the group, but temporarily he may need individual attention through the counseling relationship. It may be noted that individual counseling is not an end within itself but must, if it is to be truly effective, equip a person for wholesome group living in which his eventual state of security is to be realized. In short, unless one can come to feel at ease, adjusted, adequate to meet the issues of living, within the family, neighborhood, and other primary groups, he will never experience social and emotional security. And a higher level of security, from the Christian perspective, entails spiritual security within the communion of the Christian fellowship. Without this fellowship, one may hardly expect ever to grow into genuine and valid security.

Having said this, we should add that countless persons are in some wise related to the Christian communion who, nevertheless, suffer from a lack of spiritual security. And lack of it means that the sufferer is also very likely to be devoid of social and emotional adequacy; which means that he is basically uneasy, guilt-ridden perhaps, ill fitted to consort with humankind and consciously or unconsciously unable and unworthy to commune with God. For communion with God always depends upon being at home with one's self, just as proper self-regard is required of one before he can enjoy harmonious relations with other persons.

Mrs. Conn was discouraged and in need of help. In her church she had never found essential primary group relationships. Although she came to worship services, and occasionally dropped in for parents' meetings and other affairs, she remained unaided at the deep levels of her own and her family's needs. But by means of a particular parents' meeting she did find incentive to seek out the counselor and ask for help. Although the company of other mothers and fathers was not for Mrs. Conn a group in the sense that she felt *herself* to belong as an organic part, the setting of the parents' discussion did in this instance move her to enter into a counseling relationship.

Mrs. Conn: I've come because of what you said: " The church must be a gathering of persons who bear one another's burdens." And I have burdens.

Counselor: Tell me about them.

Mrs. Conn: It's my child. . . . He just sits in school and daydreams. He says it's no use . . . he can't learn. Says he'll never amount to anything.

Counselor: He's discouraged.

Mrs. Conn: Yes. And the reason . . . My husband; he's impossible. I don't know whether I should leave him, for the sake of the children.

Counselor: You wonder about leaving your husband.

Mrs. Conn: I have wondered for a long time. And the children have had trouble with him for years. My boy is nine. He wants to stay at home, with daddy. But the younger child says, " Mother, why can't we go away where we'll not be bothered? " I just don't know what to do. What about divorce?

Counselor: You've wondered about divorce.

Mrs. Conn: For an awfully long time.

Mrs. Conn revealed many aspects of her family situation. Clearly she had no serious intention of leaving her husband. Their tensions were of long duration, but in her mind the advantages of remaining with Mr. Conn about balanced the advantages of leaving him. In some respects the children needed even this father. Nor would she be able to support her children by working outside the home and still be in the home to care for their needs. Also, Mr. Conn was not well. He too needed her, although over the years what love she had had for him had died. Her own parents had been divorced, and her girlhood had been torn by divided loyalties. She had not had many dates, for she had known very few men. When Mr. Conn courted her, she had all too quickly married him, romantically impelled by his record of wide travels and Bohemian life.

Counselor: You were married after a few months of acquaintance with Mr. Conn?
Mrs. Conn: That's right. I did not really know him.
Counselor: What about your readiness for marriage?
Mrs. Conn: I had no preparation for marriage. Since then I've read books, all kinds of books. I know what the books on marriage say, but they don't seem to help me.
Counselor: Your understanding of the role of a wife hasn't proved adequate.
Mrs. Conn: That's right. My mother had never told me anything. I guess I was too young to be married — at least not grown up enough.

Mrs. Conn was seen five times. Twice she reopened the question of divorce, but she never revealed any real desire or intention to take this step. When unusually difficult relations arose with her husband, she grew despondent. But she would rally, and on the whole she evidenced a remarkably optimistic outlook. Obviously this optimism was only surface-deep, and she needed to talk. She reported that Mr. Conn had no desire to come for a conference. But if he could not be helped, at least their son might be encouraged to do better in school.

The counselor learned that the family had formerly gone to a psychiatric clinic, and with Mrs. Conn's permission he contacted both the social worker and the psychiatrist. Also he talked with the son's guidance official at the public school. Tests at the clinic indicated that the boy could do average or better than average work, but neither the school tests nor his performance there showed up satisfactorily. However, it seemed clear that he would improve in school once the pressure at home could be lessened. To this end he was given play therapy, and during the months that followed both the quality of his work and his attitude improved.

The son's improvement was reflected in his mother's improved feeling, but the key to success in the counseling with Mrs. Conn was hidden in the questionable extent to which she might permit herself to be helped. On one occasion the conversation went as follows:

Counselor: You say that your love for Mr. Conn is dead.
Mrs. Conn: Yes, he killed it.
Counselor: He killed it?
Mrs. Conn: We've not lived together as man and wife for four years.
Counselor: Um-m.
Mrs. Conn: I think I'm neurotic. At least that's my conclusion after reading books on psychology.
Counselor: You don't live with him as his wife.
Mrs. Conn: Never, since the night he paid me — in money. That's what I got for letting him come to my room.
Counselor: That was humiliating.
Mrs. Conn: Terribly humiliating.
Counselor: And sex is a distasteful experience, in your past.
Mrs. Conn: I could not endure it.
Counselor: Um-m.
Mrs. Conn: I tried to be a good wife to him, at first.
Counselor: At first you did have intercourse, but it did not mean much to you. Is that about the situation?
Mrs. Conn: How could it? I knew nothing about it. I thought I loved my husband when I married him.
Counselor: You wanted children?

Mrs. Conn: I suppose so. I don't really know. I love my children now, but we have an awful home life for them to grow up in. No wonder my boy is unhappy so much of the time.

The counselor might have pushed forward the fact that she did not want to become Mr. Conn's wife, or anybody's wife. Maybe another counselor would have pressed harder by confronting her with reality, but had this been done, she might have become incensed and thus spoiled her child's opportunity to have the help he was getting. Furthermore, Mrs. Conn was, from her viewpoint, getting just about what she wanted: a bit of relief by talking about her family difficulties. To push beyond that extent might simply have added to her already heavily burdened life, for it was highly doubtful if she could carry the responsibility of mature married conduct. But at least she was trying to be a good mother, and in this effort both she and her boy responded well to the help provided by the church.

III

When children are in difficulty, they cannot, of course, use words with the facility of adults to express their fears and resentments. But by means of the play interview they can get considerable relief. It is highly important, if not essential, for the parents, or substitute parents as the case may be, to be a part of the therapeutic process. In fact, in many or perhaps most instances, if re-education of parents takes place, there is little need to deal directly with the child. But children from broken homes — and from turbulent homes where the parents are unwilling to seek counseling for themselves — can be helped within the limits of the situation.

A call from a settlement house girls' worker asked if the church counselor would see seven-year-old Sara. Her parents had been divorced for about a year, and the child lived with her grandparents, who were old and ill; she not only wet the bed at night, but wet herself repeatedly during the day, at school and at the settlement house.

Tubby Sara came with Miss Grady, the girls' worker. They and the counselor sat around the tables with the play equipment, augmented in this instance with dolls. Sara drew some pictures and flitted from one set of materials to another while the girls' worker and the counselor chatted and modeled with plasticine.

Sara showed considerable dependence on Miss Grady, but quickly became friendly with the counselor and offered to sing some songs — when she learned that the electric recorder would enable her to hear herself speak or sing.

The songs she sang were strictly juke box. Her simulated "blues" voice was startling to hear, for already her childish treble was ruined. But Sara was delighted with what came out of the recorder. She enjoyed her visit to the full, but aside from the recorder only the crayons and drawing paper held her attention for any length of time.

Miss Grady: Sara, would you like to come back next week, so that you can play and make some more pictures?

Sara (continuing her drawing and giving the counselor a quick glance): I'll come if you come, Miss Grady.

Miss Grady: I don't know if I can leave the club to come next week.

Sara: I'll come if you come.

Counselor: Maybe somebody else will bring you.

Sara: My aunt might. Then I'll come.

Counselor: Would you like to come?

Sara: Yes, I want to. I like it here.

The appointment was made by Miss Grady, to be confirmed by Sara's aunt, who would, in any event, telephone the church secretary.

The following week Sara came, in company with her aunt. She took delight in showing her aunt, Mrs. Cones, around the room; then she wanted to sing more songs. After she heard them played back, she seized crayons and drawing paper and began to produce neat but restricted and uniform designs across and up and down sheets of paper. Her idea of form was limited to short, up-and-down lines of open triangles and to circles, which she traced by use of a checker. For variety she changed crayons to get different color effects. When her attention wandered, the counselor told her that she might play with the dolls. But after grabbing one and another, she put them down and returned to the crayons and to her uniform patterns.

Counselor: You may keep on with your crayons, Sara. Your aunt and I are going into the next room for a few minutes for a talk.

To this Sara objected. Her aunt promised that she would not be long, but Sara insisted upon following her into the outer conference room. At this point the counselor told her firmly that she must wait inside while her aunt talked. She went, complaining that she did not want to do so. Once or twice she appeared in the doorway, crayons in one hand and her other hand in her mouth, as if she were uncertain as to whether her aunt might go away and leave her.

Mrs. Cones: She hates for me to leave her.
Counselor: I'm glad you could arrange to bring her today.
Mrs. Cones: I get along well with Sara. Her mother was no good. It's a good thing my brother divorced her. My mother, Sara's grandmother, where she lives, tries hard to look after the child. But my mother is so crippled. Children get on her nerves.

Mrs. Cones was married, childless, and living with her husband. Both worked. Sara visited them on week ends.

Mrs. Cones: When she is with me, she never wets the bed. I would like to take her to live with us, but my husband says no. I hope you can help her to stop wetting the bed, and her clothes too.

Counselor: We can try. It seems that her parents' divorce has disturbed her.

Mrs. Cones: But she has always been a bed wetter; only she is worse now, wets during the day.

Counselor: We must try to give her security by showing her much affection. It seems to help her to visit in your home.

Mrs. Cones: Yes, she does well when she is with me. And I really like her.

Further details followed about Sara's mother, and the physician's examination of Sara (there was no organic cause for the enuresis), and the conference was over. Back in the inner room Sara rushed over to her aunt and whispered something, her face a wreath of secretive smiles, almost smirks — beyond her years.

Mrs. Cones: You can tell it out loud, dear.

But Sara did not want to do so.

Mrs. Cones (to counselor): She thinks that you called me into the other room so that I can get a divorce from my husband and marry you. This child is awfully confused about marriage and divorce.

Counselor: No, Sara. We were talking about other things. Your aunt told me about your parents' divorce, and about how your grandmother takes care of you.

Mrs. Cones: That's right, dear.

The child was watching the counselor and her aunt attentively. She seemed reassured.

Counselor: And your aunt tells me that she and your uncle will be having you for more visits in their home.

Mrs. Cones: Yes, dear, we like to have you come. You are a good girl. (To counselor) Isn't she a good girl?

Counselor: She is a very friendly girl, and I am glad to have her come here.

Sara: Can I come next week?

Counselor: Yes, if your aunt will bring you.

Mrs. Cones: Sure, I'll bring her. Won't that be nice, dear?

On the next visit, by arrangement, Mrs. Cones stopped briefly in the conference room and then left for a half hour of shopping. Sara readily turned to the crayons, though after a time she switched to the dolls, not without suggestions on the counselor's part. Enough dolls, of varying sizes and shapes, had been brought into the room so that Sara might reconstruct her family life and engage in dramatic play — if she so wished.

Counselor: You might name the dolls. One could be your mother, one your grandmother . . .

Sara: This one is my aunt — where has Aunt Rebecca gone?

Counselor: She has gone shopping. She'll be back in half an hour. Look, see my watch; when the long hand gets here, Aunt Rebecca will be back.

Sara: I can tell time. (Turning to the dolls) This one can be the father.

But after naming the dolls she was at a loss as to what they might say or do. Nor did she follow through with any of the leading ideas that the counselor offered. Her imagination appeared not so much absent as confused by the reality situation in her life. The counselor tried another tack.

Counselor: If the dolls don't want to say anything, you may do whatever you like.

Sara: Have you got a jump rope?

Counselor: No, I'm sorry. I'll bring one next week. Would you like me to do that?

Sara: Yes, I want you to.

Counselor: Tell me, of all the people in your family, or of all the people you know and play with at the club (the settlement

house), which ones do you like best?
Sara: First, my Aunt Rebecca.
Counselor: You like her better than anybody?
Sara: Yes, better than anybody in the *whole* world. And next I like Miss Grady.

Next to Miss Grady, Sara rated her father, then her uncle, and then her grandmother, finally her mother. Then she went over the list again, this time leaving out Miss Grady and putting her father in second place. Both times she placed her mother last. But when given opportunity to talk about her mother, she had nothing to say. The conversation next turned to friends and playmates at school.

Sara: I have a boy friend, no, *two* boy friends. They're silly. I have a girl friend — *lots* of girl friends.
Counselor: It's nice to have girl friends and boy friends.
Sara: And most of all I like my aunt.
Counselor: Yes, and your aunt likes you — very much. She told me so.
Sara: I know she likes me.

There followed some spontaneous running around the room, with simulated rope-jumping. Mrs. Cones returned, and arrangement was made for a visit the following week.

On this visit Sara showed herself very much at home. She did not at first ask for the jump rope — which had been brought — but busied herself flitting from puzzles to marbles to dolls to crayons. She then went into the outer room and tapped on the piano, singing in her off-key husky little voice while Mrs. Cones took the opportunity to report that Sara had stopped wetting her clothes during the day, and was having infrequent accidents at night.

Counselor: It is important to her that she can rely on you. You are first on her list of people she likes.
Mrs. Cones: I wish I could take her to live with me.

Counselor: Her week ends with you seem most helpful.

Mrs. Cones: My mother does what she can for her. But it's hard on her — she is so old. Worst of it all is that Sara is supposed to see her mother occasionally. That always upsets her. She is worse when she comes home.

Counselor: She wets more often after visits with her mother?

Mrs. Cones: That's it. But what can I do about it? I tell my brother (Sara's father) she ought not to visit her mother. But he is easygoing.

At this point Sara returned and asked if the rope had been brought. She then entertained her aunt and the counselor with her jumping performance, vigorously bobbing about the room and singing to herself until she was breathless. The counselor and the aunt praised her for her jumping skill.

Weekly visits followed over a span of about two months, until summer vacation. Sara's enuresis stopped, but she continued to make frequent trips to the toilet during the day. Miss Grady reported by telephone that Sara had had an important part in a May party production at the club. Sara was filled with pride as she talked with the counselor about the party. She thrived under this recognition that Miss Grady had provided. She continued to be reassured that her aunt liked her and that she might come to see the counselor in the fall, after summer recess and her planned camping experience. At no time was any mention made of her bed-wetting. She was shown friendship and reminded of what she could count on from her aunt, Miss Grady, and others. Sometimes she had ideas about the dolls, but what little use she made of them revealed none of her inner feelings.

It helped for Sara to be given lollipops on some of her visits, and she glowed when she found her drawings on display on the mantel over the fireplace in the counseling room. She could not easily decide which of them she wanted to take home and which she should leave to be displayed for other children to see when they came for visits to the church.

It will be observed, from this account, that greater help should have been given Sara. Her father refused to come in to talk, though he had his sister make an appointment. It probably would have been better, had it been possible, for Sara to be taken into her aunt's home. But as time passed, Mrs. Cones reported that she was showing continued improvement. Had the counselor been able to talk with the father, an agreement might have been reached by which Sara could have been told enough of the facts about her parents' divorce to eliminate most of her confusion on the subject. This would have supplemented what was done (and that proved helpful) to reassure her about the affection felt for her by her aunt. Miss Grady's work at the club was of pronounced assistance to Sara. And, not least in importance, her opportunity to see the counselor (at first just another strange man) talking and meeting in a normal way with her aunt served to dispel some of the child's earlier images gotten in her home. For from her infancy she had seen a series of strange men coming to her mother while her father was away at work.

IV

It is evident that counseling varies in value from situation to situation, from person to person. What the counselee brings to the conference — what he is deep inside — the quality of his mind, the kind of damage, and the extent of it previously done to him as a personality, plus what he really wants — these determine, far more than the competence or incompetence of the counselor what the end results will be from the counseling sessions. One might almost say that most of us, at some period in our lives, need counseling — particularly those who are professional workers. Just as the psychoanalyst is required, as a part of his training, to have psychotherapy, so the worker with persons — the minister, the teacher, the physician, the personnel officer — might well have counseling. Much of this work would be in the nature of preventive emotional medicine. Much of it would uncover problems too complex for the nonmedical counselor to handle.

Because people normally spend most of their lives in groups — in families, neighborhoods, clubs, businesses, and the like — and because conflict induced by what is often called personality clashes is too often the order of events, individuals remain immature unless they discover the therapeutic value to be derived from counseling. It is in personal relations, among their fellows, individually and in groups, that persons either erupt into open antagonism, verbal and other kinds of warfare, or fall into fatal withdrawal, or else learn to live maturely.

When the spiritually insecure person feels unfriendly toward himself, when he is laden with anger of long duration and his fears have accumulated and grown into a pervasive anxiety, he has to break out against something or somebody or break down and enter psychotic oblivion. If Smith bawls out Jones in their office, with slight provocation, the chances are that Jones merely happened to be available for Smith's purposes of explosion. It need not be the case, nor is it the case many times, that people clash because their particular personalities do not jibe. Most explosions have a history frequently more or less unrelated to the particular moment that one of the Smiths happens to erupt in anger. But every Smith among us is making it indubitably clear that he is in need of the therapy that generally is available in the conference room of the worker with individuals who can deal with the ordinary problems of life. And if Smith is found to be in need of more specialized counseling, or other therapy, the step from the counselor's room to the medical clinic, or to the psychiatric couch, is shortened by virtue of the fact that he has already elected to seek out his pastor or teacher for help.

It would seem the better part of wisdom for the disturbed person who aspires to reach spiritual security to seek the assistance of a competent counselor. And every disturbed child deserves to have his parents, or other adults close to him, take him to a series of play therapy sessions. But after therapy there remains the larger phase of guidance: that of relating the individual to the religious community that may advance his growth in spiritual security. Just what organized Protestantism might do to meet this responsibility is our concern in the next three chapters.

5

THE CHURCHES FROM A COMMUNITY PERSPECTIVE

❦ ❦

CHRISTENDOM purposes to design a community transcending institutions that retard or degrade man and prevent his entering into a realm rightfully his. But theists with a holy vision, believing in a personal God, and humanists, with no God or an impersonal one, have proved themselves unable to transform the transient kingdoms of this world into a deathless Kingdom, the Blessed Community.

Churches are only partially fulfilling their mission to redeem individuals and society, and securely root human personality in the divine. The Roman Catholic Church is true to its philosophy when it tries to absorb within its regimen tight control of family life, education, and all aspects of public morals, including political control. But in trying " to pertain to the whole " (Holy Catholic Church) it claims *to be* the whole — the whole of truth — only to demonstrate repeatedly its presumption, its institutional effrontery. At its heart there is too much pride and dogmatism to enable it ever to set the design of the Blessed Community.

The ecumenical movement among Eastern Orthodox and Protestant Churches offers a design for drawing truth from " each household of faith." The movement's culmination (Amsterdam, 1948) in the World Council of Churches does not mean that its supporting denominations have crystallized as a single organization; they are a council, a federation.

As this movement seeks to draw from various households of faith what may be hoped to be the genius of each, with none claiming to have the whole design of truth, a fellowship may arise, higher than any possessed by any one or all the Churches added together, worthy to summon humanity to its banner. This is high hope which arises both from faith and from need; it is voiced by a philosophy which sees truth possible only as it derives from many truths.

The science and art of human relations, as represented, for example, by intensive group appraisal (see groupness report), sociodrama, counseling, and the like, have their contributions to make toward building the Blessed Community. And if churches in the local community were willing to lose their life in order to find it they could join with social philosophers, social scientists, and thoughtful laymen to tackle the job of developing at least a Protestant pattern available to a community that is looking toward realization of the new community in which men might be blessed with abiding security, a community to which something of the City of God might come. Practically speaking, this means that denominational organizational structure must give way to interdenominational thinking and administrative procedures that take account of the ecumenical purpose. The first step toward this end is an inventory of the local Protestant community, and that will probably have to be taken by laymen.

I

Look at your community. It will seldom divide so neatly, but it probably has the equivalent of churches that we may call Meetinghouse, Stone Church, Red Brick, Modified Gothic, and Parish House. All these churches represent different denominations and each has a minister. Of the five ministers, all can preach reasonably well and some believe in the ecumenical idea that their seminaries have been emphasizing. One has special interest in Christian education for children; one shows skill in youth work; one is strong on social justice; another reflects his training in pastoral psychology and is sought after as a counselor; and one is a superior salesman and promoter. All these men are attempting to give their separate churches an inclusive ministry. For all it is difficult to find time to study and to be with their families. Each minister tries to enter fully into the numerous constructive affairs of the community.

The new council of churches in your community, an outgrowth of the ministerial union, is promoting weekday religious education, mainly because most people recognize that the Sunday school is inadequate. It is hard to raise the money for weekday religious instruction and next to impossible to find enough well-trained professional teachers. A tedious meeting reviews the situation: Meetinghouse is paying its share of the assessment. Stone Church is behind because its members are already giving all they can to the fund to renovate its sanctuary. Red Brick has little real interest in weekday religious education because its minister, though an able educator, believes that the expanded Sunday teaching schedule of his parish is a better answer to the problem of sound Christian training. The other churches are unwilling to put up money until they are sure that competent teachers will be in charge.

As the ministers talk, now and then pausing to allow the laymen to speak, it becomes clear that the five churches, instead of starting out to make full use of their existing Sunday educational programs and ministerial talents, have resorted to the popular weekday movement without due deliberation.

Whether the minister-led council of churches is dealing with Christian education or with other issues of common concern, what it seeks is co-operation — and that is not enough. Churches today cannot be content merely to operate together. If they are to do the job that must be done to meet the needs of man and fulfill the will of God, they must be *co-ordinated* — of one order. If ministers have performed the valuable service of charting the way of interdenominational co-operation, it remains for laymen to move forward to co-ordination. To illustrate:

The minister of Modified Gothic, a competent counselor, might by common consent open his office to all who wish his help. He can then concentrate on counseling and general priestly functions, leaving educational leadership to the minister of Red Brick. He need not spend himself in trying to get the high school youth of his congregation to attend his Sunday evening group; for those youngsters are flocking to Parish House on Sunday evenings, to join their public school friends who belong to that church. Besides, Parish House's parson understands them; they like his approach.

So far as the needs of the Protestant community are concerned, the Parish House minister would make the best contribution by devoting most of his time to youth. He can direct a program that avoids too much division among the young people of the various churches and at the same time points them toward the particular church of their parents. When adolescents of five churches attend the same high school, it is contrary to their herding habits to insist that they support five separate church youth organizations. Furthermore, if Parish House is wise, it will use its renovation fund to found a community church camp, a youth chapel, or a library of religious books that will meet the needs of adolescents and adults alike.

The chances are that at least three of the five churches in your community are planning to spend enough money to provide at least three times as much church space as the local Protestants need or can afford. Available funds might better be diverted to strengthening the work of the World Council of Churches, to promoting missionary enterprises, to expanding relief programs around the world. Purposes of this high nature would stimulate the local Christian community to renewed zeal and bring it a spiritual awakening the like of which it will never know so long as the churches foster ingrown and puny objectives.

There are obvious arguments against these suggestions. Some people will say that churches are not yet ready for coordinated work. But it should be equally plain that they can get ready by starting. And the starting is up to laymen. Other people will contend that laymen are just as much habituated to the old ways of Protestant divisiveness as ministers. But times are changing. In a less complex society, when the church offered about the only means for individuals to express themselves through positions of leadership, it would indeed have been futile to advance proposals for a unified Protestant community program. But modern life makes so many demands on people, offers them so many opportunities for self-expression through leadership, that they do not have to maneuver in the church to gain prestige. Civic and social outlets drain off this self-seeking energy — partial vice that it is — so that the real problem of the local church is generally to find enough leaders to fill the jobs, instead of multiplying church jobs, as formerly, to meet the demands of parishioners who want to stand in the spotlight.

It follows, then, that laymen are very nearly ready for coordinated community church work. But the venture will have to be a *community* venture, undertaken by people who already have communion in some areas of human relations. People who now enjoy face-to-face relations in parent-teacher associations, in the public library, on recreation fields, in civic promotion, and in business, are probably ripe for unified church work. And they will start it the moment a solution appears to the problem of finding competent church school teachers, financial canvassers, and the like.

Laymen are not without a chart for this work, for church councils have long held interdenominational training classes for Sunday school teachers. If an educational method is good for the children of Meetinghouse, it may be as good for the children of Stone Church. If visual aids promote better learning in one church, they may be relied on by the next also. If the pastor of Red Brick knows how to enlist and train competent teachers for his own church, he will probably be able to serve the entire Protestant community equally well. And while he is freed for this work, his promotional duties can be carried by his fellow minister who takes over the united promotional task of the five churches.

Skeptics will point out that this proposal assumes that there are no doctrinal differences left to divide Protestant churches. If Gothic Church preaches a near-humanism and Stone Church prays to Jesus, the two will certainly find it difficult to merge their emphasis in a unified program for educating children and youth and counseling individuals. This is something of a problem. You may lose one or more of the five churches in your community as you move toward co-ordinated objectives. But whatever number remains, use it. You may confidently expect that, when it next makes a ministerial change, the particular church now out of line is going to have as its parson a man who is more sympathetic toward the doctrinal views that now prevail in your community.

It will be said that these proposals logically call for a weakening of denominational over-all bodies and mergers of two or more of your five churches. Well, what of it? Do denominational overhead bodies exist to serve the local church or vice versa? A more essential question is, Do local churches owe their first allegiance to denominations or to the Body of Christ?

Actually, however, it is possible that your community will find it more advantageous to keep five churches than to merge some of them. The exploratory discussions may even expose an undeveloped area of the community where an additional church is needed.

Co-ordinated local Protestant work looks toward inclusive community service and at the same time allows ministers to specialize. In most instances, all the ministers will continue to preach — at least once each Sunday. Thus each church will retain its immediate fellowship through the worship experience. Most of the priestly functions will be performed as now. But the teaching of children, work with youth, family guidance, individual counseling, church building programs, social action, community reform, and participation in the World Council of Churches will become unified and comprehensive enterprises instead of the separate and sketchy activities that they now are.

In place of a one-man staff in each of five churches, there would be a five-man staff operating as a unit among the Protestants of the community. And the individuals composing the staff will find that their effectiveness is increased when they come to act alone.

Of course it is likely that the Protestant ministerial staff in your community will not, at first, be so nicely balanced as to talents and interests as in the imaginary community we have been picturing. But the community council of laymen and ministers will quickly perceive the necessity for making future staff appointments in the light of the comprehensive program. Many ministers, like other professional men, want to work in situations where they can specialize. Suspicious laymen may continue to think that all clergymen conceive of specialization as preaching. That was true until recently, but modern ministers have broader interests, in keeping with the more varied training programs in the seminaries and the trends of modern society. The minister remains a preacher, but he is quite happy to have means of expression other than, or in addition to, the pulpit.

Tired ministers, too long spread thin, need relief. Fractional Protestantism needs wholeness. Co-ordinated work in the local community can cut waste to a minimum while providing a comprehensive program. Laymen have experience in planning and carrying through co-ordinated enterprises much more complex than this kind of co-operative Protestant approach. They can undertake this long-term and inclusive program for their communities. And they must do so if Protestantism is to make its contribution to the local community, helping to design the Good Society in which persons may gain the religious stability and spiritual security too long denied them.

II

" How can the church hold its youth?" When a parson or someone else concerned with the unpredictable behavior of young people asks that question, he has to be told the shocking truth: " It can't."

A church cannot hold what it does not have. If it had its youth safely within the fold, it would not need to ponder how to keep them there. If they are truly in the church, they are there because it has drawn them in, appealed to them, touched the deep places of their needs, and woven them inseparably into the fellowship. There are churches that accomplish just this. There are far more that blunder and sadly watch those between the ages of twelve and twenty-four abandon the churches of their childhood, the spiritual home of their parents, for the fellowship of the peer group — wherever it leads. (Years later, some return, religiously illiterate, wistfully or dutifully bringing their children to the nursery class.)

If a young person's peer group abides with the church, in most cases he abides. If it forsakes the church for satisfactions that can be got only outside the church, he too will often forsake the church. The plain fact is that temporarily or permanently most young people give prime allegiance to persons of their own age. Devotion to the group precludes (temporarily or permanently) conformity with parental wishes in respect to church, excludes the claims of the church, and often cancels out childhood devotion to God. Consequently, much of the group life of youth, being outside the church, causes young people to suffer from spiritual insecurity.

An overstatement, in some instances. The problem is not that youth are atheists. Recent investigations at Harvard and Princeton offer reassurance that youth today are not godless. But Luella Cole, the psychologist, surveys numerous studies of youth and religion and concludes that modern youth, though socially and ethically sensitive, are destined to become almost completely divorced from organized religion. Valid or invalid, this prophecy should warn that studies of the religious attitudes of young people have turned up enough evidence to give sectarian protagonists pause. And should anyone desire very much to know what adolescents think of religion and of religious leaders — parsons — he can go to no better source of information than the book *Elmtown's Youth*, by A. B. Hollingshead.

Both the careful student and the casual observer of the

religious situation among young people agree that youth grow increasingly impatient with denominationalism. Many of them are politely immune to a church that, in a scarcely veiled manner, seeks to gather them in as fuel to stoke the dying fires of an organization cold with sectarian antiquity. Alert young people definitely refuse to be exploited by a parson or lay leader whose motive and proffered program are aimed at feeding a starving institution instead of gratifying the spiritual hungers which modern youth still have. It is worse than futile to plead, " Your church needs you " — meaning, " Unless you come, we will not have a live youth organization or a suitable numerical report to make to denominational headquarters. "

If these pleas are futile, youth know equally well how trifling is the argument that maintains, " The church will die unless young people bolster it by attendance and loyalty. " The harsh truth is that critical young people do not particularly care whether the local church lives or dies. And of the Church Universal they have but the faintest notion, if any. It is beyond their ken — perhaps because the local expression of the sect has obscured the Church.

But we must not be unmindful of the mass demonstration of youth's allegiance to the Church at such gatherings as the World Conference of Christian Youth at Oslo, Norway (1947), and the United Christian Youth Movement at Grand Rapids (1948). Neither should we forget that many local churches over the nation are now enjoying the fruits of effective appeals and decisive Christian challenges to young people. A few years ago the American Youth Commission studied 13,500 young people, using Maryland as a representative state. Three out of four claimed church membership. Protestants showed up less favorably than Roman Catholics, yet 39 per cent of the young people from Protestant homes regularly attended church. This is encouraging. Likewise encouraging is the evidence that many veterans of World War II have a more active interest in religion than they had before their war experiences. Nevertheless, it is clear that institutional religion is acutely unsatisfactory to great numbers of war veterans and other young people alike.

It may be contended that young people are today less religious and more ethical than their parents and grandparents were in their youth. They are less religious in the sense of being less bound to the Church. But they are potentially religious in the sense of holding in readiness high devotion to a Christian fellowship that transcends the sect and its instrument, the denominational church.

A young person, more easily than an adult, finds his church connections at the community and group level rather than at a sectarian level. He operates within a community context, not within a denominational sphere. Churches might as well realize this and admit that no conceivable Sunday evening variety show can equal the force of the appeal of the group with which a young person habitually consorts. Free dinners and similar bribery by his home church avail little when an adolescent knows that his clique are headed for another church. It is not entertainment that such a young person seeks; it is communion with his kind, by means of which he may later commune with God.

Not every church can provide the sort of adult leadership that will command the respect and loyalty of a group of young men and women. The group seek and move about until they find a minister or a lay sponsor whose kinship with them is genuine, whose quest for justice and truth is, like that of youth, fresh and growing. If one church in a community of a dozen churches has the right adult leader, that church should be encouraged to specialize, ministering to youth of all the churches. Thereby the eleven churches are enabled to specialize in other areas of Christian service to the community. This is a boon, did churches but know it. This is wonderful, did overworked parsons but realize it. For every parson to strive to become expert in youth work is almost as pointless and impossible as if every man should try to master the principles of atomic energy.

Adolescents tend to be uncomfortable when their numbers are few. Accustomed to move in flocks during five school days a week, they feel bereft if caught in a handful on Sunday. It is an elementary fact that few churches actually know how many youth are available within their membership for their youth groups. A bit of stocktaking ought to help pastors and official boards to appreciate the wasted effort involved in trying to pressure young people into " going out and bringing in more members." This approach often serves to drive out the few who are already in.

Sponsored by the rapidly growing number of councils of churches in American cities, youth work at the community level is slowly taking shape. Quarterly, or more frequently, churches are bringing their youth organizations into a single gathering, thus presenting something of a united front while retaining separate societies or youth fellowships which continue to meet in their respective churches on most Sundays. This procedure presupposes that the separate churches have competent leadership and that their young people actually respond to the home churches. If the system works, if the youth like it and support it, well and good — for the present. Yet the fact has to be faced that there are too many struggling youth groups, just as there are too many churches. The life of the separate organization is complicated by denominational programs, literature, and rallies; by interdenominational projects, planning committees, and mass meetings; in short, by a clutter of organizational machinery which is over-emphasized to the detriment of spiritual development. The whole affair quickly becomes predominantly promotional, eating away at energies that ought to flow into creative development of persons and the Church of Christ. Not spiritual growth and personal security for individuals but organizational vigor is the order of the day.

Ask thoughtful leaders how they reconcile the dual approach of denomination and community and they are silent, baffled. Ask the opinion of young people and their decisive shrugs indicate confusion or displeasure. Undoubtedly there are values in providing for the small, intimate group within the home church while at the same time uniting with other groups on special occasions. But this means that an eventual choice has to be made between two valuable systems: quasi or full ecumenical youth work. The dilemma has to be solved according to the local situation. No general recommendation will suffice, but it should be clear that a dual approach to church youth work is presenting two masters to be served — the home church and the community of churches.

The reluctance with which churchmen advance Christian unity — whether with adults or young people — stems from clerical fears that denominational strength, local and national, will diminish. But it is by no means certain that Methodist youth who meet on Sunday evenings with Congregationalists, Presbyterians, and Disciples at the Baptist Church in the Protestant Youth Fellowship, will automatically become Baptists. Granted that some risk is taken, it is likely that the young Methodists will continue — or begin — to attend their church for morning worship, and do so with added desire by virtue of having discovered within the inter-denominational experience new meaning in Methodism.

The validity of this observation might well be put to the test!

On the other hand, the question has to be asked, as it must always be asked when serious consideration is given to modifying sectarianism with ecumenical ventures: If the churches are unwilling to lose their lives, how can individuals ever find their lives under the aegis of organized religion?

The *Program Guide for Interdenominational Youth Action* and the study pamphlets — published by the United Christian Youth Movement affiliated with the National Council of Churches — are replete with ideas for ventures in religion. Both the U.C.Y.M.'s organizational proposals at the local level and its outreach toward a world Christian community connote essential simplicity, unification, and experiences for which youth long. Practically speaking, the U.C.Y.M. could replace denominational organization (the static) with Christian movement (the dynamic). However, it is not the objective of the U.C.Y.M., or of any other branch of the educational division of the new National Council of Churches, to replace denominational programs. But it should presently become clear that if youth are to be guided toward the heights of Christian experience and service, diffused efforts eventually may need to be supplanted by a single inclusive Protestant program. Encumbrances now stifling the Churches must be shaken off, or Christendom will remain ungirded for the imminent battle to the death with secularism and insecurity.

Perhaps some of the money now being spent on denominational youth work should be diverted to help to provide adequate leadership and equipment for all the communities of the nation. But before that can happen Church presses and national boards must put an end to their competition and wasteful duplication of materials, program, and field services. Once realistic unity of effort is established, seminary students will begin to prepare for a ministry to youth in community terms. Once official church bodies determine to assess youth's needs and community resources to meet these needs, funds will be diverted from denominational channels to feed Christendom's common reservoir.

If and when concerted youth work is established, it will probably not be because of vision so much as because of necessity. The educational level of the population is at its highest in history, and public education may be expected to offer progressively finer resources in personnel and equipment. Sterile churches cannot keep pace, for their appeal to youth is vanishing. And unless they recognize their ineffectuality, their days are numbered.

On two fronts youth are ready to advance: on that of community organization and on that of meeting personal and group spiritual needs. Under the latter heading a philosophy and a faith born of Christian essentials, not sectarian trivialities, can emerge that will be satisfying to the soul hungers of modern youth. When that happens, doctrinal and Scriptural investigations will follow upon youth's demands. Primarily activistic, youth still yearn for theological dimensions which they have seldom found within the limits of churches whose principal exertions have been thrown into sheer survival. So far as American youth are concerned, the denominations with their separated churches need to give up their lesser claims to the higher demand of the Church Universal as the Body of Christ. Were this to happen, youth could find within Christendom real hope of spiritual security and social redemption.

Hearty disapproval of organized religion as it is can be the motive power to establish religion as it might be. Complacent church members, parsons and laymen alike, are fatal to the life of a church. They reveal no capacity to grow in the grace and knowledge of either God or man. But when people come in their dissatisfaction to face together the weakness of their religion, there is cause for hope. And when we find that the best human, secular schemes and devices yield little hope for achieving personal satisfaction and social salvation, we are ready to venture into a fellowship in which we accord the Father of Jesus a central place; there is the beginning of a new fellowship that can provide us with spiritual security.

III

The churches use religious education as a principal method for propagating themselves and for nurturing growing persons. The aim is life with God, now and always, for the individual and society; and the belief is that this life is imparted to those who enter into fellowship with Jesus Christ.

For the most part, the educational work of the church is conducted along denominational lines only; seldom is a community approach made to the task. Although religious education on a sectarian basis is inadequate both in conception and in design, that is the way matters stand. However, the present system does offer hope for improvement, structurally and religiously. It may be said that organizational improvement is but preliminary to more effective nurture in spiritual development. Our main concern is with the heart of Christian nurture — the growth of persons — but we do need to give some attention to certain trends apparent in the educational work of the church.

For over a hundred years in America, with few exceptions, churches rather than schools or other institutions have provided programs aimed at bringing up the younger generation in a way of life calculated to embrace the meaning and truth of human existence. In recent years religious education within Protestantism has been attempting to move forward on at least five fronts. It seeks extended time for teaching, improvement of leadership, released-time and other devices, educational evangelism and church-family education. Does any one or any combination of these efforts give promise of more fruitful times for this portion of the church's program?

Modern religious education can be dated from the rise of the social gospel early in this century, the coincident development of educational psychology, the founding of the Religious Education Association in 1903, the inauguration of the graded lesson idea shortly thereafter, all these soon followed by the beginnings of vacation church schools and released-time or weekday religion during the first and second decades respectively of this century. During the latter half of the period since 1900, churches here and there over America have considered — and some have actually tried — a plan for extending church education beyond the time limits of the traditional Sunday school. It is argued that more time for teaching means more learning and better teaching methods. Some, not many, curriculum materials have made provisions for what is called, in a swelling phrase, " the expanded session."

No one knows what percentage of the churches of the country enjoy — or struggle with, as the case may be — the lengthened Sunday morning period. Judged by the infrequency with which sign painters have been called upon to revise announcement boards in front of churches, it would seem that no popular movement has arisen in favor of a two- or three-hour Sunday morning school in which children engage in a variety of activities supposedly connected with Bible and related studies. Observation of schools that have added to their hour program leads one to conclude that too often the so-called activities period has little or no relation to the content of the more formal lesson period. Relatively few children attend the extra period. Teachers are inclined to fear it and parents know little about it. Church boards do not seem to get sufficiently stirred up over the idea to allocate adequate funds or to provide a suitable plant.

We must conclude that too many factors combine to stifle any very serious effort to establish a two- or three-hour Sunday school. The idea always has two strikes against it: first, the fact that it is hard enough to get teachers for one hour without adding to the recruiting burden by asking prospective teachers to serve for a longer period; and second, the fact that more time inevitably means more money. Solve these two problems and there can be considerable justification for placing confidence in the expanded session idea. Until then we cannot look for much from it.

Then there is improvement of leadership. Through what was formerly the International Council of Religious Education (now the Division of Christian Education of the National Council of Churches), leadership education has been extensively promoted. So far as the number of courses and training schools is concerned, there is cause for satisfaction. And if interest in the accrediting system for lay teachers is not so great as it might be, there are distinct gains in other plans. Particularly noteworthy is the workshop method. Although professional religious educators are making more use of workshops than are laymen, there is reason to expect that greater use of workshops for lay teachers lies ahead. If so, this augurs improved church education.

Nevertheless, at least three main problems must be solved before churches can secure adequate professional and lay leadership: (*a*) The gap must be closed between the present demand for professional workers and the available supply coming from our seminaries and schools of religious education. This issue is closely related to the problems of recruiting and training teachers for public education and ministers for the churches. Space permits only a recognition of the persistent need to develop long-range plans for guiding selected youth of secondary school age toward specialized service in religious education. (*b*) Seminaries must train students to teach as well as preach. Christian education will always be dependent upon the ministers. In *The Pastor and the Children*, by Mildred and Frank Eakin, there is a valuable treatment of the issue. (*c*) Lay educational workers must be recruited at the community level for service across denominational lines. This is not a reference to interdenominational training schools. More than these, interdenominational Sunday schools are needed. At this point only bare suggestions can be offered.

Let us remind ourselves that churches tend to cluster at certain corners in our towns and cities. Proximity favors united Protestant Sunday schools. The history and tradition of the Sunday school movement favor interdenominational lay co-operation. Yet obviously, as demands for better teachers increase, the available number of competent persons declines. Six churches in a cluster can hardly find six sets of good teachers, all of whom have to be drawn from a single community. However, out of this community *one* set of good teachers might be expected to be available for an interdenominational program.

Difficulties crowd this suggestion. To mention only one — a practical one — it may be asked how a single staff of teachers could handle all the pupils from six churches. One answer is that, given a thoroughly educational performance by a competent teaching staff, there could be higher standards required of pupils before they could enjoy the privilege of attending the school. Higher teaching standards would facilitate the handling of larger classes. At the same time there would probably be fewer pupils at the outset. And, to be realistic about the issue, there are not many Protestant homes ready to fulfill the requirements for participating in a genuine school of the church. But no matter what the difficulties and objections might be, at least one creditable Sunday church school could be established to replace the existing six makeshifts. In this connection the plan used by Protestant churches in Oxford, Ohio, should be investigated. (See *International Journal of Religious Education*, July–August, 1948.)

What about released-time and other devices for strengthening religious education? Released-time religious education continues to be warmly debated. Whatever one's views may be about this plan for releasing children on school time, at the request of parents, for an hour or more a week to study in the church of their choice, one must agree that the national picture is a very irregular one. Two convictions may be stated about released time: (1) It has reached the zenith of its development and therefore it will never solve the problem of providing the growing generation with adequate religious education. (2) It is just as well to look for better plans, for sectarian overtones and the smearing of the boundary between Church and State raise potent objections to the released-time idea. In this connection, Conrad H. Moehlman's argument merits study. In his book *The Church as Educator*, he indicts released time on fifteen counts, the last of which repeats the thesis of an earlier book — *School and Church: The American Way*. Dr. Moehlman holds that released-time religious education " promotes the disintegration of public education." He insists, moreover, that public education as offered in this country is " the only valid approach to religion in the American way of life."

A considerable body of those in general education may

agree, but religious educators are likely to have other ideas. No thoughtful religious educator wants sectarianism injected into public education. Dr. Moehlman correctly holds that the public school can teach ethical values and conduct. But there is growing insistence that the American way allows for another approach to religion in public education. One may hazard the guess that an articulate portion of the 86,000,000 Americans of all faiths associated with religious bodies of the country are ready for a fresh examination of the relation of Church and State in education.

The study *The Relation of Religion to Public Education — the Basic Principles*, made by F. Ernest Johnson and his associates for the American Council on Education, finds that the early struggle over religion in our public schools "was a contest over sectarianism, not over the importance of religion in education." This document makes a strong case for the belief that it was never the intention of people like Horace Mann to separate religion and education. To the extent that there exists in our schools today what the Johnson study calls "negative religious dogmatism," we actually have an un-American practice.

The American Council committee is bypassing released-time religious education and is asking that public education engage in a study of religion, integrating it with the social sciences and literature. The committee proposes that sectarian indoctrination be avoided, and that the study of religion be conducted in its proper setting as a part of the culture and history of man. The purpose of this proposal for improving religious education is clear: "It is the business of public education to impel the young toward a vigorous, decisive personal reaction to the challenge of religion."

The 1951 publication of the Educational Policies Commission (1201 Sixteenth Street, Northwest, Washington 6,

D.C.), *Moral and Spiritual Values in the Public Schools*, makes the point that the schools "can and should teach about religion."

One prophecy opens the way for another. If one may predict the decline of released-time religious education, one may be allowed to hail the ascendancy of a public-school-sponsored study of religion. It is the "study of religion," not the act of "teaching religion," that Professor Johnson and his committee (and also the Educational Policies Commission) are stressing. This is the task of public education, and this is religious education. But *Christian* education, as indoctrination, will still need to be carried on in the home and church.

So now we come to the fourth of the current trends in religious education. How fares educational evangelism? Many educators in the field of religion understandably take a critical view of evangelism that appears to require a more or less sudden decision for Christ on the part of the young. They could hardly be within the tradition of Horace Bushnell and do otherwise. It was about the middle of the last century that Bushnell declared his now famous belief that "the child is to grow up a Christian and never know himself as being otherwise." Nurture is a basic doctrine in religious education, and it is not likely that its force will soon be spent.

But nurture has not functioned effectively enough to keep the educational program of home and church healthy. Among the very denominations that have made the most extensive use of modern teaching methods, enrollment and attendance records have sometimes proved disappointing. Actual loss in enrollment in some Sunday schools or failure to keep pace with the national population growth has made religious leaders wonder about the future of certain Protestant churches. A static Protestant birth rate would not help matters. Add to these conditions the outbreak of World War

II and it is easy to see how the door was readily opened, in 1944, for beginning the National Teaching Mission, a plan to promote educational evangelism through the Sunday school.

An adequate analysis of educational evangelism would be too extensive here, but it should be said that a main objective of this movement, among the co-operating denominations, has been to reach unchurched children, youth, and adults for the purpose of enlarging the Sunday schools. This is in part an effort to evangelize children by instruction — instruction gauged to the level of the child's development. Commitment to Christ is sought when the individual has readiness and understanding.

More basic than the problem of reaching additional participants are such questions as to how nurture and conversion are to be harmonized, how Christian teaching and proclamation of the gospel are to be balanced, how children are to become Christian, and not merely " enlisted," before parents are evangelized. Probably most religious educators would be the first to welcome an insistence on evangelism were they more confident that the apostles of this movement had as their principal objective the conversion of adult sinners whom the gentler and more gradual methods of education have failed to reach. A procedure that fails to reach adults first, that fails to deal with the family as a unit, can be expected to produce only limited results. Fortunately, however, churches are beginning to plan for guiding the family, as a unit, in religious living. There is much cause for hope from this direction, as we shall see in the next chapter when we examine the fifth trend in religious nurture.

6

CHURCH–FAMILY RELATIONS

❧ ❧

THE FIFTH of the current trends in religious nurture, mentioned in the previous chapter, deals with Church-family relations, which can be educative in the deepest spiritual sense. We need to be very clear as to what we are here considering, and so we must look briefly once again at just what the Church is, for the quality of its fellowship should become that of the family also.

I

Essentially the Church is a fellowship, though we generally persist in thinking of it as an institution. Of course it is an institution, firmly fixed in society. And it is many more things besides: a company of believers in Jesus Christ, the Body of Christ, the communion of saints, both invisible and — we still hope — sometimes visible. But principally we must bring into as clear a focus as lies within us the essential meaning of the unalterable fact that the company of Christian persons who constitute the Church, and from whom lasting security is derived, is a human and divine fellowship. The word fellowship has been so overworked as to lose its best meaning, but we need to restore its meaning by examining it afresh.

Just what, precisely, *do* we mean when we speak of the Church as a fellowship? We mean that it is made up of persons who recognize in each other so great worth that the significance of the Church can be grasped only when people remember that their fellow Christians are sons and daughters of God. In any context, fellowship entails a sense of mutuality, which means that the discerning person knows that people in fellowship are expressing conscious or unconscious interdependence. But in Christian fellowship, not merely human relationships are lifted up to the high level of appreciation of persons one for another. Christian fellowship reaches the highest level attainable by human beings who freely admit the Spirit of Jesus Christ to a communion which then is no longer simply human, but has become both human and divine. This is certainly true when God in Christ, through the Holy Spirit, is impregnating persons, permeating human relations so that man's respect for man turns into devotion, and human admiration turns into love of the brethren. Briefly put, when we are in and of the Church, we know the high worth of our fellows and we experience the supreme joy and meaning of communion with Almighty God himself.

Like the Church, the family also is a fellowship. Again, like the Church, the family is a social institution, a basic and primary one. But well we know that both Church and family, times without number, are broken and shattered, so that their nature is negated and their very existence disrupted. Yet, when the worth of persons is seen, when people so value each other as to experience joy, patience, long-suffering, gentleness, sacrifice, and love, they are drawn together as a unity from which envy, strife, selfishness, and pride are banished. In the family that is bound together by interactive love, the individual finds a sure sense of belongingness. In this realization, even by means of merely sensing this security through love, a member of a family derives social stability, psychological integration, and is well on his way toward the

wholeness essential to spiritual security. As family fellowship
embraces also the Spirit of Christ, it becomes in microcosm
what the Church is in macrocosm.

Here before us are two spiritual fellowships: the Church
and the family. But we are not to think of them as existing
side by side. They are not to be considered as standing in or
functioning in a parallel relationship, for this would mean
that they never meet. It is incorrect to imagine that they can
exist independently. They are never to be viewed separately.
Let us not even speak of the Church *and* the family; rather,
you will note the hyphen joining the words " Church-family " as they appear on these pages. That little ink mark signifies that Church and family are linked — but the linkage de-
noted by the hyphen is hardly an accurate representation of
the greater meaning in the truth that these two fellowships
really flow together, really interpenetrate, so that it is truer to
think of them as being not two fellowships but one. That is
why the mechanistic concept suggested by the necessity of
printing the words " Church-family " with a linking hyphen
is both an inadequate and a false concept. For the fellowship
that is imbued with Christ's Spirit as found in the true
Church and in the true family is a single fellowship. It is one,
though it is operating in two phases on the human scene.

Church-family relations are effected by means of an educational process. This education does not take mere knowledge as its chief objective; rather, it aims to inculcate in
growing persons, as learners, both the grace and knowledge
of Christ as Saviour and Lord. It is as a by-product of such
education that the learner may experience spiritual security.
Church-family nurture clearly signifies that this nurture
takes place within the Christian fellowship — a fellowship
ordinarily regarded as confined to the Church, but which, as
we have seen, is within Church and family alike. Necessarily

we should not conceive of Christian education by the family and the Church, which do not merely " serve and support each other " as two separate agencies; they can have their essential existence and meaning only as they interpenetrate, thus becoming one, just as the vine and the branches are one.

Before Church-family education can be established, considerable pruning of dead branches of Church and home relations must be undertaken. Clearly there are unfruitful offshoots from past mistaken and halfhearted overtures to the families of our Churches. There is the dead branch of parent co-operation. That is not at all what is needed, for the idea underlying this oft-repeated and relatively futile plea for co-operation is that the Christian Church is the chief — perhaps the sole — teacher of religion. It has been assumed that parents can safely turn over to the Church the whole of the responsibility for the religious growth of the young. Recent radical departures from this false assumption are pointing the way toward reinstitution of the family to its place of equal or greater importance in the teaching of the Christian faith. However, most of the Churches' educational programs continue to call merely for parent co-operation. If the Church and family are by nature one in fellowship, and if nurture within this Christian fellowship is the way in which spiritual growth in the grace and knowledge of our Lord takes place, then it is assuredly not mere co-operation by parents that is required. What is required? Obviously it is essential that the family shall become a center of spiritual living, consciously striving to make the Spirit of Christ manifest, just as the Church, if it be true Church, seeks to do. But can the family be, as it were, a little church within the larger local church? And what is the parent — the local church — to do in order to insure for its child — the family — a spiritual level of living equal to its need to become a valid expression of the Church of Christ? That is the great task and challenge to which Christian education leaders are responding in increasing numbers. Their job is nothing less than that of seeking to use the local church as a matrix in which to start, fashion, and nourish as many little churches — Christian fellowships — as there are families within the mother, the local, church.

This is a most difficult undertaking, but one which may presently receive the greatest amount of attention within American Christianity. How, indeed, can our glaringly faulty church fellowships find enough strength and health for themselves so that they can give birth to the infinite progeny suggested by the idea of the Church's forming and sustaining families until they can mature and become churches themselves? Is not the Church too exhausted already to dare to undertake the rigorous course of bringing forth more progeny?

What, in short, must leaders now undertake before Church-family education can be established? The educational program of the Church will have to be redesigned so that the family unit rather than the individual is the pupil. This point will be amplified presently, but it should be stated in passing that the churches have too long joined with other agencies that have been guilty of misconceiving the way in which persons learn and grow. Like other agencies, the churches have split the family group, dividing its members and enlisting them for age and interest groups almost completely to the exclusion of any possibility for the family to participate as a whole within the church. Furthermore, the church programs often leave families little opportunity to live and learn as Christians together in the home. Let us, accordingly, get rid of the dead branch of custom which divides families in as many directions as there are individual members.

Before churches summon families to the rigid requirements of a Church-family program it would be well for them to make a careful study of the homes related to their parishes. This calls for a careful census, the gathering of enough information to guide any steps that might be taken toward enlisting homes for Church-family education. Let us be rid of the dead branch of ignorance about our church families.

And we must know our particular community. Any serious attempt to transform a church into a genuine fellowship requires that we understand the economic, social, class, and political structures that influence and in a large measure control the lives of people. We have to be realistic about the class and caste divisions that exist among church members. Community forces, the dynamics of group relationships, cliques which govern adults and youth alike, have to be taken into account as we try to make Christian love function. The exclusiveness so easily detected outside the Church can also be seen operating within the Church. And when persons are not led to face up to the motives, desires, prejudices, and customs which bind them into rigid patterns of behavior that restrict and sometimes destroy fellowship, they will never be free, never become creative enough to experience fellowship within the Church.

Assuredly the Church has to make of itself a communion of love before it can break the bonds that hold fast the people outside its fold. For church members largely reflect the modes and values, the customs and allegiances, of nonchurched people. We must know, therefore, what these phenomena are before we can deal realistically with our problems, thus freeing ourselves for creative fellowship in which church and family may experience the meaning of spiritual communion. Our goal is nothing less than that of correcting the irreligious patterns of our communities. But before we can essay that job we have to assess the character of the community and rid ourselves of the dead branch of vagueness about our communities.

II

Now what will Church-family relations look like when they are established? It is evident that specific programs sometimes reveal many things of either secondary importance or of actual worthlessness.

First, certain churches are trying to promote parent-teacher associations, but the P.T.A. idea is not for the churches. In the schools this organization undertakes to acquaint parents with what the school is doing for the child, and it sometimes gets the parents into study groups and service projects for the welfare of the school. Only in a very limited sense is there any conception of the interrelatedness of home and school as a joint establishment for the education of the child. Furthermore, the P.T.A. in the public schools has no thought of unifying home and school so that the two shall become one teaching order. Because the church P.T.A. assumes that it is to be like the public school P.T.A., let us disavow it for the church. Let it stay in the school. When we have Church-family education, much more is operative than a P.T.A.'s functions. It is not simply child education that we seek in the church; it is family education, which means parent education first, so that out of the overflow, and hence naturally and most effectively, parents may teach Christianity by living their faith. Church-family education means that children learn to be Christian by seeing their parents earnestly and consistently strive to live up to the ideal of the Christian faith.

Example mainly, some precept — never too much precept — is the function of parents. Not only so, Church-family education, unlike parent-teacher co-operation in the public school, calls for church teachers and home teachers unified, co-ordinated as fellow teachers of the young. It is not co-operation that we are after; it is much, much more: it is co-ordination of church and home, which means teachers of one order.

Secondly, there are innumerable sporadic and superficial efforts now being made in the churches — in the weak phrase often used — " to interest our parents." And by use of the word " parents," mothers are generally meant. So it is that afternoon teas are held and the mothers listen to yet another invitation by some church leader "to come and visit the church school; see what is going on." To be sure, we need the mild conviviality of tea-drinking in our churches. No doubt far better official board meetings would be held if the church fathers took to drinking tea. But the danger is that tea parties will squander the energies of church teachers and disappoint parents who accept the invitation to visit the church school and get acquainted with what is being done. Often these parties denote the sort of educational leadership that has not thought through the problem of where church education is headed. Such gatherings lead straight to parents' disillusionment. When they find no basis for their aroused hope that professional church leaders can equip them to nurture their children spiritually, parents are worse off than before they learned to expect the church to help the home. Instead of urging parents to join with unprepared leaders and teachers, fathers and mothers should be asked please to stay away until it can be determined what it is the church is prepared to do with the family, particularly with parents, once they are actually ready to work under professional religious leadership.

Thirdly, some churches are sponsoring family fun nights, to which children, youth, and adults may come for a supper, games, and other entertainment. Assuming that people need recreation and that they come willingly, this is fine — provided that in addition there is provision for parent conferences with ministers and teachers. No doubt fun nights at the church are a step toward wholesome fellowship as well as recreation. But if Church-family education is to be realized, the adult participants will have to guard against being content merely to play together.

Fourthly, parents' classes, especially when planned by members and when held in response to evident need, contribute to Church-family education. The main trouble with formalized classes for parents is twofold: they seem too often to depend on intensive promotion by church officials, instead of arising out of parent-teacher conferences in which recognition is gained that parents must study if they are to guide the Christian development of their children; and they seem inclined to play around with every item of child care except the heart of the Christian message. Adults have to be Christianized before they can guide children into the fullness of the truth of the heritage and faith. Family health, recreation, diet, and the like can be made relevant to Christian nurture, but the danger is that beyond these items many classes may not go.

Fifthly, family worship services are becoming a main aspect of churches that have awakened to the values that inhere in enabling young and old to gather in the sanctuary. Family worship requires far more careful planning and execution than the ordinary adult worship service. It is more difficult to conceive and conduct. In practice it may range from reversion to the family-pew idea, which subjects children to ideas beyond their comprehension, to repetition of children's day "programs." To put children, individually or by church school departments, on display and have them speak a piece to the delectation of adults — or to the extreme embarrassment of parents and teachers alike — is to miss the value to be found in a significant family worship service. This service has to depart from either of the extremes just mentioned and offer a design not for exhibition but for worship. When conducted in the right way, family services can draw old and young together not only in the church but also in their spiritual living at home.

It will have been noted ere now that it is not so much that these undertakings in Church-family education are either secondary or worthless of themselves; some of the things being done can retard, some advance Church-family relations; some are unimportant and can yet be made highly significant. So it is that due preparation must be made for parent-teacher conferences in which a unified teaching order faces the mutual and distinctive responsibilities of home and church. All parents' teas, family nights, parents' classes, and worship services must be channeled into a single drive to make Christian fellowship operative in church and family. The organization to be used should come from the local church's philosophy of what Church-family education is in spirit and what it can be operationally. It is not schemes that should occupy the churches, not plans for high pressure promotion, not mere adoption of some new curriculum — however desirable that may be for a given church. Primarily Church-family education is a relationship in which the church and the home find that each belongs to the other, and both belong to God, whose Spirit makes true fellowship possible and insures thoroughgoing spiritual security for the individual.

III

What can Church-family education accomplish? Reference has been made in Chapter 3 to Burgess' and Locke's assertion that a major change in family life replaces the individual's subordination to the group's welfare with individualism. One might say that this is a polite way of observing that we are more selfish, less given to sacrificing, in family relations than formerly. But we must not forget the favorable facts that marriage has remained popular; people are marrying at an earlier age; larger flocks of children toddle over the land than at any time in our history; and serious students of family life agree, in the main, that the future state of the family is bright; social disintegration is not to be our lot. Take the dark side and the bright side of the family picture — look at both and add your own observations. The tensions, insecurities, and other evidences of rootlessness that pervade family and social order alike, justify the conclusion that a new core, a spiritual center, is desperately needed by the American family. If Church-family education is anywhere nearly as promising as it appears — both as an ideal and as a potential achievement under the leadership of the Churches — it can provide the unity and spiritual reality that homes must have if families are to remain families. In short, Church-family education can cure a large part of our social ills and restore spiritual security to lonely and fearful persons. Unbroken families can be strengthened and broken homes can look to the Church to supply spiritual foster parents.

The Church fellowship might give attention to providing neglected children with substitute spiritual parents. The Big Brother Movement ought to be proof enough that it is possible and concretely helpful to befriend children whose homes are deficient. Families are smaller than in past generations. Childless couples and small, intact families can find point and purpose to bearing one another's burdens in Christian fellowship, if plans are developed whereby children of broken homes are related to unbroken families for certain experiences, yet are able to continue to live in their own homes. Furthermore, as Church-family programs evolve, always indigenous and responsive to the democratically led Church, opportunity and need will be found for the fellowship to compensate for the religious deficiency of many unbroken homes. Just as good schools work harder with problem children than with well-adjusted children, so the Church will have to do more with children from religiously irresponsible homes than with those from homes where Christian fellowship prevails.

Church-family education can bring church teachers and home teachers together in a continuing relationship wherein the child's spiritual growth is seen to involve the family first and last, and the parents are viewed as needing the fellowship of the church as a fountain needs a reservoir. Church-family education can help the family to understand and to discharge its primary function as a school of living. And the Church can be transformed, by means of Church-family fellowship, released from its present plight of reflecting the social order so as to undertake, in daring freedom, to change the social order. Under the aegis of the Church, families can learn how to share decisions, learn how their members together can confront a world that is wont to pull person from person, shattering family life. In regular parent-teacher conferences, held at least once a month, fathers and mothers can be guided, under the professional leadership of the church, to think of every significant choice and major crisis as their opportunity to deliberate and grow as Christians with their children. The whole family can decide how — as Christian stewards — to use income, skills, time, and talents. In the very act of making a decision, the family unit will learn to take action in which the requirements of God expressed through the ethics of Jesus are truly lived by. It is possible for God, not conventionality, to cause a family to stand against racial discrimination, against local and wider injustices. When parents study the church school subject matter used with their children, they can understand what they may have missed in childhood and youth, namely, that Bible materials and all religious ideas are worthless save as persons dedicate themselves to fellowship aimed at making Biblical truth functional.

The main accomplishment of parent-teacher conferences does not lie in enlistment of parents to serve as supervisors of homework assigned by the church school. The home is not to act as a monitor for the church. Nor is Church-family education a device for tightening the lines between home and church so that children cannot get by with any misdemeanor or negligence. Family and church teachers may not rest content to collaborate on improving the character of the growing person. More than all this is called for. What is needed is not incidental parental interest but essential parent education. We want our children to abide by the Christian ideals and actions that they learn in the church. We know that for most of them to do so, parents must be helped to find Christian fellowship and thus throw their weight against social cleavages, class distinctions, racial discriminations, and merely respectable religion.

Church-family education can Christianize the young and old. It can turn homes into centers of Christian living. It can become a principal medium for redeeming the social order and making individuals secure, for it is rooted and grounded in love which sees high worth in human interrelations, which sees supreme worth and meaning in fellowship elevated to communion with God.

How is a program of Church-family education to take place?

IV

George Heaton, minister of the Myers Park Baptist Church, Charlotte, North Carolina, started with the recognition that the Protestant minister must teach as well as preach. Dr. Heaton has taught high school students, and his associate minister teaches junior high pupils. These two large classes are broken into separate grades during a part of each Sunday morning for the purpose of testing students on the teaching done in the home during the week. Adult sponsors — the equivalent of assistant teachers — conduct the tests and prepare monthly reports which are shown to parents. The ministers have found that parents will study with interest the same lesson themes that their children are studying. In this church, at chosen periods of the year, from 150 to 200 fathers and mothers of high school students meet on Sunday evening to investigate the Bible (from the point of view of modern Biblical scholarship), using the same material that their sons and daughters have had in the morning classes.

Regular conferences are held by departments, attended by parents and teachers who strive to improve themselves as teachers engaged in a joint responsibility for Christian nurture of the child. Family nights each week, attended by young and old, provide food, prayer, and fellowship for strengthening family and church alike. Pastoral counseling follows naturally from these varied experiences shared by ministers and laymen, by church and family.

Parents receive regular reports on the progress of the child in the church school. The psychology department of a neighboring college is used to test students. The church office has on file cumulative records, with information that is made available to colleges to which students apply for admission upon graduating from high school, *and* from church school. The student's respect for this system is as apparent to the visitor as is the conviction of the adults that in and through participation in their church, home life is being solidified, enriched, and given a purpose exceeding that found in the ordinary Christian family.

The First Church of Christ (Congregational), West Hartford, Connecticut, has emphasized nursery education. For a number of years, under the leadership of Mrs. Vincent J. Maramarco, formerly director of religious education, parents engaged in study aimed at making the home a living and learning experience consistent with Christian faith and the principles of child development. Mrs. Maramarco's work was based on the belief that if the church is to help the home to nurture children, the educational program within the church itself must be strong. Her article " A Conference with Teachers " (*International Journal of Religious Education*, March, 1949) shows how church education thrives by means of educational counseling.

The First Methodist Church, Schenectady, New York, under the leadership of Dr. Leon M. Adkins, the former minister, has placed importance upon parent groups' studying both the child and the principles of Christian education. Classes for young children are so conducted as to provide adult participation, whereby parents can observe their children's relationships with their group. The objective of home-church guidance is aided by a locally prepared guidebook, and other materials. Periodically parents meet in the church lounge for discussion and study. Familylike atmosphere is encouraged, with books all around and coffee at intervals.

In the churches cited, parents have responded to ministerial leadership that is committed to the educational function of the church. Moreover, these churches operate with full understanding that laymen ultimately determine whether or not the church can serve persons at the point of their need and interest. In these churches men as well as women are alert to their opportunity to learn how children become religious. When they can get definite help from the church, men will assume their role as religious guides of their children. " How Does the Family Teach Religion? "; " How Shall We Teach Children to Pray? "; " How Attitudes Are Formed "; " Recreation in the Christian Family "; " Parent Answers to Children's Questions " — these topics illustrate how churches are drawing in parents.

One church, not mentioned above, set out to implant a program of Church-family education by printing family enrollment cards, announcing parent-teacher study groups and other features taken from what was thought to be a model church. Needless to say, the result was something less than salutary. Any departure from traditional methods has to be inspired by a democratic decision to investigate the local situation. A minister or lay leader will do well to sit down with his present church school staff and analyze the existing program. He will ask: " What are our aims? To what extent are they being realized? What are our problems? How can we solve them? "

Assume that the teachers of the primary department are baffled by rowdy pupils, or by the unsatisfactory way in which the children respond to class sessions. Decision may be reached to study the nature of children. Any minister or church school superintendent can profit from a book like *The Child from Five to Ten,* by Gesell and Others. With the teachers and parents of the primary children he can enjoy weekly sessions, for at least three months, spent in mastering the studies reported in this book.

After general study parents and teachers may advance to a study of individuals. (Simple and helpful is the manual *Individual Parent-Teacher Conferences*, by Katherine E. D'Evelyn, published by the Bureau of Publications, Teachers College, Columbia University.) A parent may soon perceive that an eight-year-old is balking at church school attendance because his mother sabotages religious activities. A teacher might come to see that certain children can scarcely be expected to express reverence for God so long as infelicitous parents are irreverent toward each other. A minister may find that a nervous and erratic seven-year-old is a victim of repressive handling by a neurotic father. Teachers, parents, and ministers will come to grips with the inevitable necessity that child guidance be conducted by means of family guidance. And family guidance is up to the minister.

Seward Hiltner's book *Pastoral Counseling* stresses the author's belief that no minister need doubt that he can learn to counsel. *Pastoral Counseling: Its Theory and Practice*, by Carroll A. Wise, admirably shows what the task comprises. Serving people requires individual and family guidance. The pastor-counselor will know his limits and stay within them. He will know when to refer mentally ill persons to psychiatric counselors, but, as his people find him reliable, he will be astounded by the dimensions of the area in which he can work as people face the fears and faithlessness that characterize the times.

Those who are ready to reorganize the educational program of their church to embrace the family may consider the following proposals which summarize what has been suggested above:

1. Hold a family worship service six or eight times a year. Give over the entire morning service to music, Scripture, prayer, and story as nearly as possible within the range of understanding of the youngest children. Omit the usual adult sermon, use children's and youth choirs, weave into the worship service litanies and prayers developed by church school classes or by families in the home. Use young people to assist with the reading of Scripture and the leading of prayers. This plan will get parents to church who would never come were not their children bringing them. (The Congregational [Community] Church, Winnetka, Illinois, uses this plan effectively.)

2. Have a family dinner one night a month. Meet early, provide recreation suitable for young and old. Use original entertainment and, when possible, films, slides, and drama suitable for the family. (Consult the audio-visual department of your denomination, or the Christian Education Division of the National Council of Churches.) Adjourn at a reasonable hour for the sake of the children's sleep.

3. Concentrate on a particular age level, experimenting with a department of the church school for two or three years. During the fall of the first year have a week-night meeting of parents and teachers, not less than twice a month, as a combined staff; thereafter confer at least once a month. Examine the plan by Muriel Streibert Curtis, " Christianity Begins at Home " (one of the last productions under the Commission on Marriage and the Home of the Federal Council of the Churches of Christ in America; inquire of the National Council of Churches). Let families report on their experiences in following this plan in learning to worship and rendering service to the world of need. (Numbers of churches are doing this.)

4. Define, within the experimental department, the responsibilities and opportunities of the home and those of the church for teaching children religion. Make a thorough study of how attitudes develop in children, and acquaint adults of all existing organizations in the church with the results. Pamphlets from the Bureau of Intercultural Education have been found valuable for parents and church school teachers.

5. Organize the experimental department so that one teacher becomes a personnel officer to:

    a. Observe the conduct of the children and get additional information from parents and schoolteachers.

    b. Make anecdotal records of individual children — what they say and how they adjust to their group.

    c. Note special contributions and promise of leadership.

    d. Advise the home and each pupil about his work in the church school.

    e. Pass on information to the minister about symptomatic behavior, thus using the child as an index to the family's need for conferences with the minister.

6. Lead the religious education committee or board of deacons in finding through observation what the current developments are in church and home education. The merits and demerits of the Union College Character Research Project (see *A Greater Generation*, by Ernest M. Ligon) and the curriculum for home and church developed by the Presbyterian Church in the U.S.A. will likely serve to make local church leaders more confident that Church-family education is most genuine when it arises through their own purposing and planning.

7. Let the church that is experimenting consider these objectives of Church-family education:

    a. To improve the teaching in the church.

    b. To acquaint parents with what the child is being taught.

    c. To enable parents and teachers to understand that the home is the most influential of all agencies in determining the attitudes, values, and conduct that shall characterize the growing child.

    d. To enlist parents for regular participation in at least one aspect of church life — so that children will begin to perceive that their parents are themselves concerned with religion.

    e. To provide parents with books, magazines, devotional materials, pertinent lectures and discussions, and other aids for living the Christian religion.

    f. To help the home to become positively Christian in atmosphere and conduct.

    g. To make easy the conversation within the family about religious experiences that the whole family has had in the church.

h. To teach the family how to make decisions in all areas consonant with the Spirit of Jesus and the Christian ethic.

8. Expand, in due time, the parent-teacher conference to include the entire church school. As experience is gained with monthly conferences, a demand will often arise for weekly, short-term study groups to go more thoroughly into religion and child guidance than can be done in monthly gatherings. The principle should be rigidly followed that activities for the sake of activity have no place; they must be sponsored by the church only as the people are ready for them to meet their specific needs.

9. Adapt your present curriculum to Church-family use. Church-family education requires no sudden importation of a lesson series wholly different from whatever series is in use. Almost any educationally and psychologically sound textual materials can be adapted to unify church school teachers and parents. Out of their regular planning conferences, to which are brought church school experiences and vivid accounts of family councils, family recreation, service, and worship, will emerge a living curriculum — a program vital and reliable. The object of Church-family education is not to mechanize family life or fasten it rigidly to a time-consuming program held in the church. Neither is our purpose that of causing parents and teachers to " gang up " on the child so that he finds himself an object for psychological conditioning. Rather, Church-family education seeks to unify home life around shared experiences brought to a level of spiritual devotion and ethical living.

10. Keep your program of Church-family education flexible, responsive to human needs, democratically expressed. Operate with the conviction that the church exists to support the family as it seeks to live for the glory of God. The family must not be exploited to boost church organization. Let it be repeated here that *Church-family education is a relationship, not a scheme for putting over some particular program.* For this reason, original, creative, local development is essential for its establishment.

In the Christian fellowship the family comes into its richest experience, and within the nurturing relations of the family, as a fellowship, the individual finds enduring security.

7

WHEN FAMILY AND CHURCH ARE ONE

❧   ❧

IN THE BOOK *The Church and Christian Education*, Paul
H. Vieth presents the conclusions of a two-year study
made for the International Council of Religious Education
by a committee of sixty educational and Church leaders.
This committee is not satisfied that Christian education is
operating as united Protestantism, in its 1940 statement of
basic philosophy, has said that it must.

For example, curricular materials have given too little
recognition to the place of the home in guiding the religious
growth of the young. It is now time for Christian educators
to concentrate on "growing Christians," to use Vieth's
phrase. This means that we shall give less attention to promoting church schools and more attention to the way in
which persons learn to be religious. And the way we learn,
what we learn, the faith that we come to possess, and the conduct that characterizes us, depend more on our homes than
on any other single agency. The importance of the family is
primary. So far as most children are concerned, we can teach
them to be religious only as we first teach adults to be religious.

The goal of Protestant teaching has been too much concerned with giving information to the individual, to the
exclusion of causing him to grow spiritually in his natural
groupings. It cannot be repeated too often that the basic

group, in and through which a person learns, grows, and indeed comes to be a person, is the family. If we would reach individuals for Christian nurture aimed at mature commitment to the person of Jesus Christ, we must aim for the family unit. And this — despite the exceptions noted in the last chapter — is seldom undertaken. Many leaders say that they would like to deal with the family in a fresh and vital way but do not know how. How does the leader begin?

I

Mrs. Norman H. Erb, director of religious education at the Old South Church, Boston, has used a striking method which she calls " group conversations." Mrs. Erb and the minister, Dr. Frederick M. Meek, have long been deeply concerned that the church shall empower the family for its mission of nurturing the young and old in genuine Christian faith.

For a high pitch of interest in group conversations, few groups can equal the mothers of children in the weekday church nursery class. But two limits are essential for a group of young mothers: (1) No more than eight to twelve should be included in any session; and (2) adjournment must be planned to coincide with dismissal of the nursery class, else a terminal point may be reached with exceeding great difficulty.

It is instructive to note that mothers revel in these sessions, principally because they do the talking. (This is not in the least meant to be a slighting remark.) They *should* have the opportunity to talk. In truth they are doing plenty of it, at random among neighbors and friends, during the mysterious and intriguing days when their toddlers are turning into little boys and girls very much with purposes of their own. The mobility of our population has left too many young mothers bereft of access to their own mothers and fathers, aunts and uncles, nieces and nephews, all of whom would ordinarily be contributing to the young parent's education in how to bring up children. The scores of excellent books and pamphlets on child guidance simply are not adequate to lend assurance to the mother isolated by modern society in her task of bringing up her child.

It seems to be peculiarly true that the same mothers who attend study classes in child care also delight in informal group conversations, conversations that generally deal with the same areas " covered " in the more formal classes. Nor are mothers intimidated when a child " expert " is present to join in the conversation. When visiting specialists are prepared to give the sort of inconspicuous leadership discernible in the following accounts, fruitful learning and reassurance are bound to follow. Among the chief topics of conversation likely to be engaged in are the perennial favorites " discipline " and " how to teach little children to pray."

For instance, here is a discussion of discipline:

A Mother (who has been trying for five minutes to get her word in) : It really works, you know. It really does. I can't tell you how much I owe Dorothy Baruch for her book *New Ways in Discipline*. I even got my husband to read it.

Another: But does he practice it? Mine doesn't.

The Same: At least I got him to read it. I'm not one to demand miracles. And, let me tell you, our Bobby has already stopped sucking his thumb.

A Third: He probably would have by now, anyway.

The Same: Maybe so, and maybe not. I feel safer with Baruch lying on the table. Besides, I told you girls last week how stupid I'd been — how demanding I was of Bobby. Now I just drain off his anger.

A Fourth: Give us an example.

The Same: Well, this may embarrass somebody — me, I daresay. The other day I found myself about to deal with Bobby the way his father does — when Bobby balks, I mean. (Pause.)

The Fourth: Well, go on.

The Same: Give me time. I was in a hurry to get him cleaned up, and finish supper before my husband got home. I'd called him several times — he's so hard to pry loose from the little boy next door.

A Fifth: An only child craves a playmate *so* much.

The Same: Don't I know it. That's why I tell big Bob he's got to get busy and earn some more money — quick, so we can have the twins.

A Sixth: My, that girl hunts trouble! It's all I can do to manage Junior.

The Same: As I was saying, Bobby wouldn't come, and —

A Seventh: Do they ever?

An Eighth (the final one, save the " leader "): *Do* let her finish!

The Seventh: What's the matter, dear, are you in a hurry to borrow the latest method to get your Julie in from play?

The Same: Please let me get this off my chest. As I was *about* to tell you, Bobby yelled at me to pipe down and go drown myself, or something lovely like that. So I flared up and started to yell back at him.

The Fourth: And next you probably did what I usually do: gave him a smack on his little rear end.

The Same: No, not that, but I grabbed him and was shouting down his grubby neck — as his dad does — that he'd come and come at once, or I'd take his gun and hide it for a whole — but then, Baruch! I stopped, calmed down as cool as you please, and said —

The Third: You said, *so* sweetly: " Bobby, Mother knows you don't like to be interrupted — "

The Same: Not that way, please! I said calmly: " Bobby, you don't like to come for a bath, and I know how you feel. It *is* more fun to play out here with Johnny." I reflected his feelings, you see. Then I said, in my mature, quiet voice, that he could play some more tomorrow, but that now we would have the bath and be ready for Daddy. I took him by the hand. And in we went, as pleasantly as you please.

The Third: What, no tantrum?

The Same: Not that day, at least.

The banter drops away as the group exchange further details about the desirability that children be respected as persons who have rights, whose anger needs to be released rather than bottled up, and whose conduct must be firmly directed so that, though expression may be given to negative feelings and hostility, the child may not be permitted to destroy property or to injure his parent or any living thing.

The Seventh: Once I made the terrible mistake of letting Janie kick my shin. I was so stupid I even *urged* her to kick me. Can you imagine? She was angry with me for something I'd done, and in my naïve way I thought if I'd let her kick me that would release her feelings.

The Eighth: Just what is the difference between encouraging a child to punch a pillow instead of kicking you?

The Seventh: I don't quite know. What *is* the difference? (looking at the visiting " leader ").

Leader: Briefly, the child's anger is taken out on the pillow, which of course he knows is all right for punching; but when he senses that he has hurt a parent, guilt is added to his already aroused feelings. He always has in him at least some fear lest his parent become incapacitated, and hence unable to care for him. So we have the combined weight, in the disturbed child, of anger, guilt, and fear.

The Eighth: That's too heavy a load even for an adult to carry.

The Third: Which reminds me — what I've been wanting to know is why my five-year-old continues to suck his thumb during the daytime. We've been careful not to nag him about it. I've told him I think he's about old enough to want to stop, but he keeps right on.

The Fifth: Pressure. Some kind of pressure. Or maybe he never had enough sucking as an infant.

The Third: I did breast-feed him — for a while. But I guess you're right. It's pressure. Just the other day, when I'd been complaining to his father because we never seem to have a night out — the old problem of professional men, you know — Connie said: "Don't you and Dad get to arguing again, Mommie. It does no good. I'll take you someplace, and we'll have fun." I may have to take Connie to a child clinic, but I know my husband will object. He's suspicious of psychiatrists.

The Seventh: Better go anyway, I say. Or else you and friend husband get yourselves on friendlier terms.

The Third: I sound as if we fight like cats and dogs. I do love my husband, you know. But — but — sometimes . . .

Leader: I believe we must keep in mind that our children can respond very quickly to a smoother home climate. May I add, at this point, that by " discipline " we mean " learning "; inner control on the part of the child, so that he *wants* to do what is necessary, is our goal.

The First: Which puts it up to us, that *we* are the first and most important educators in the child's life.

Leader: Exactly.

The Third: I'm almost frightened at our responsibility for the emotional development of our kids. I surely don't want to have my child reach grown-up chronological age and remain an emotional baby.

The Seventh: It happens every day. Sometimes I wonder if I'm grown up — inside, I mean.

The First: Don't we all!

The Second: It all comes down to this, it seems to me: Discipline means learning, and most of the learning has to be done first by us. The kids are always ready to respond to the right way of feeling and doing. A child with any spunk won't behave if you try to force him, but if you have the knack of *guiding* him, his behavior will be wonderfully good. Am I right, Mr. Leader?

Leader: That makes sense to me.

II

Group conversations may indeed offer the participants surprising self-revelations and eloquent testimony to the fact that within human beings lie greater virtues than generally appear on the surface of life. The above dialogue is not a faithful record of actual conversation. Were an electric recorder used in a situation of this kind and the conversation reduced to type, the reader would have before him an hour and a half of words covering many pages. But this record, as here offered, may be taken to represent the essential content and direction of informal exchanges among persons who, not being under the restrictions of the classroom or of a " study " group, in a permissive relationship verify the fact that educational and spiritual values can be derived when the setting is right. And this record just about says what group conversations are.

In the group conversation there is no leader, in the usual sense of the word; rather, there is a convener who sets the stage, who is ready unobtrusively to help the conversationalists to move forward productively. An electric recorder might show that this group, like any informal group, used much of the time in wandering off on tangents, in making side comments, in stopping at dead ends. A moving picture camera would have revealed grimaces of perplexity, expressions of disapproval, nods of agreement, friendly smiles. Too, a sound camera might have found a steady progression from individualism toward group feeling, of aloofness at the start fading into a consensus of feeling and thought.

The native interest people have in one another, even though not well acquainted, is a factor that contributes to the zest of exchanging ideas and experiences. In this session, mothers were discovering each other, venturing together. Minds were growing through a process of sharing, reaching together toward understanding and communion. For group conversations, along this line, are both educational and therapeutic. When insights and values are explored by persons who join in facing a common problem, because they desire enlightenment instead of trivial talk, then it is that understanding is deepened. Minds grow as horizons of thought are expanded.

In any group, of whatever size and occasion for coming

together, there are likely to be some individuals who are lonely, frightened, worn by the frustrations of the daily grind. Emotional satisfaction accrues from the experience of free exchange of opinion and thought. People want to see the faith by which others live. They deeply desire rootage in hope and love. More than that, spiritual renewal is almost inevitable when the dominant mood is respect for any person and any sincere expression. Gentleness and forbearance, rather than pressure and exposure, mark the group's conversation.

It will be noted that the leader spoke infrequently. He was a fellow participant, or, to put the matter somewhat differently, he was but a leader among leaders. Each could follow at points and each was free to lead out with ideas at other points.

It is also noteworthy that this particular group, unlike most perhaps, had in it not one person who monopolized the conversation. Definitely an unusual group! And if the reader should maintain that not once in a thousand years could it possibly be true that such virtuous and superior persons might meet under circumstances of this kind, the answer can be given that more groups would approach this level were they but given the setting herein described. But if our skeptic presses the matter further and argues that no conversation could possibly sound like this, that individuals really do not talk this way, the reminder may be offered that though people seldom speak as significantly as these did, neither are the lines in a play precisely the way people talk.

Reports of most conversation groups would show a high percentage of the time taken up with direct address aimed at the most recent speaker, asking him, " How do you mean? " telling him, " I'm afraid I don't quite understand you," and with the replies of the one addressed expressing his first statement in two or three different ways: " In other words . . . ," or, " I think I mean this." Always group conversation encourages, if indeed it does not require: (1) clarity of expression, (2) careful use of words, (3) opinions that one must be prepared to back up, (4) facts that can be validated, (5) willingness to hear out the other fellow, (6) care on the part of each one lest he monopolize the time or speak dogmatically, (7) a sincere search for what is true rather than merely proper, (8) readiness to have one's belief qualified, perhaps changed and improved, by what others believe, (9) genuine respect for persons, and (10) enjoyment of an exchange and development of ideas. A high degree of rational behavior is exacted of persons who participate in group conversation, and few can take part without attaining an added dimension of maturity.

In a period of countless mechanical communications interpersonal communication is at low ebb. It is a truism that Americans have lost the art of conversation. And yet conversation between friends, and occasionally in group gatherings, remains a most natural and enjoyable human experience. However limited significant group conversations are where persons gather for one reason or another, purposeful, informal conversation, if the setup is right and the stimulation adequate, can contribute richly to personal development and emotional security. For the fact is that when minds and spirits really commune one with another, the modern individual's sense of aloneness, perhaps of lostness and aimlessness, is dispelled by the dawning of spiritual security.

III

Four couples, parents of preschool children, decided at a dinner party that the subject they had found themselves discussing toward the close of the evening required fuller exploration at a later date. One of the fathers suggested that their minister be asked to guide the group when next they met. So it came about that the group are in the church parlor trying to find an answer to the question, What is the proper way to teach our children to pray?

Each one talks at length and asks all the questions he has long had in mind. Then a mother says to the leader, " I wish you would say something more about what prayer means to you."

Leader: I've found that I can't pray unless I've set right the human relationships. For instance, I'm angry with Junior. Before I know it I violate his right to be understood and forgiven. Because he dawdles when I'm in a hurry to give him his bath, so that I can be on time for an evening engagement, I sternly order him to snap to it. He responds in kind and orders me to stop bothering him. I'm challenged, I get angry, maybe slap him or at least threaten him. I win by brute strength, get him in the tub, give him a few jerks, rush him into bed and — time to pray? Well, hardly. Junior and I might as well try to digest cucumbers when a tiger is chasing us. There's too much adrenalin in our blood to try to induce the love of God to flow into our hearts.

——: So what do you do?

Leader: I skip the forced mumbling of words that might pass for praying. Neither the boy nor I can pray; I know it and he senses it. And if I can summon enough common sense, I tell him that I'm sorry, that I should not have rushed him or treated him the way I have. If I haven't been too brutal, childlike, Junior is quick to forgive me. You know how quickly children can shift from one mood to its opposite — for example, from crying to laughing, when they are approached right. Then, because I'm forgiven, I can pray, and if I really am in the presence of God, Junior is the first to know it; and he too can talk with God, because he wants to get in touch with the unseen power who obviously causes me to be an affectionate father.

——: But if the mood for prayer is not so easily restored, what then?

Leader's Wife: Those are the nights that Dad clumps noisily down the stairs and grumbles a good-by. Anyway, when I go up to put out Junior's light I am likely to find him still awake, wanting an extra hug.

Leader: Yes. And that extra hug has to make up for the boy's loss of the love feeling I've destroyed — at least for that evening. When I get hold of myself, I realize I've caused Junior the double loss of affection for me and confidence in God, both of which feelings he must have in order to pray.

Leader's Wife: I know, but I think it's more honest for the parent who feels mean, and can't shake it off, to drop any pretense of praying until the meanness is overcome. And I certainly don't approve of just *hearing* children's prayers. That is a sure way to cheapen prayer and make it mean worse than nothing to the child — and to the parent.

Another Mother: I agree. What you say is even more helpful than the ideas I find the books offer us — to help us with bedtime prayers. The problem is to make the ideas work.

Another Father: Doesn't it all come down to the question of whether we, the parents, actually *believe* in prayer?

Leader: Yes, and whether or not we do more than just hold to a sort of *intellectual* acceptance of the reality of God, and the idea that we ought to get in touch with him — when we have a convenient moment. I go along with the view that it's a complete mistake for us to let our children get the idea that prayer is something that adults teach children to say, when they are small, instead of communion with God which grownups practice themselves, and join in with their children during their early childhood, while they are growing up, and so long as the family live under the same roof.

Another Father: I'm interested in your point that human relations have to be right before people, little and big people, can really pray. Suppose my wife and I have just had, shall I say, one of our very infrequent quarrels. If we start praying then, isn't that the quickest way for us to cool off, to restore love?

Another Mother (not the questioner's wife): Maybe it is for you. But not for me. That seems to me little better than counting to ten.

——: But I still say, the very act of praying can put us in the spirit of prayer.

..——: I can't agree. For myself, I first have to voice a sincere apology, and couple that with an attitude to match the words I use in asking my husband's or my child's forgiveness, before I can pray in the right spirit. And isn't it absolutely true that unless this is done, we not only cause the other adult, and older children in the family, to feel that we are hypocrites, but we also instill in very young children a lasting feeling that religion, God, and human love are nonexistent?

——: I see your point. And if you're right, then we are simply fooling ourselves, lots of times, when we think we are teaching children to pray. Maybe we are really teaching them to hate God, because — because —

Leader: Because we're teaching them to hate the way we parents treat each other. Is that it?

——: I don't want to put it in quite that extreme way. But I can see how forcing prayer, when ill feeling is present between the parents, or between a parent and a child, can easily become associated in the child's mind with his parents' harshness, or bitterness, or possibly just their hurried, preoccupied manner which shuts him out. Anyway you take it, the child gets so he dislikes praying; and it might mean that he would hate God — because he fears or hates the times when there's friction in his home.

Leader: That's right. That's why I insist it is better to get ourselves in tune with each other, by restoring harmony, before we dare to try to enter God's presence through prayer.

——: But don't we believe that God is *always* present with us?

Leader: We say we believe it. And so he is — present and grieving when we play the devil. When I feel like the devil, if I stop and think, I know full well God *is* present with me. That's what hurts. Sometimes the stab of guilt moves me to confess that I'm being a heel. Other times I deliberately go right on playing the devil. But the point is that in knowing God is still with me, I do not dare address him; not until I can make room inside my wretched self for his holiness to enter. To me, trying to talk with God at the very time that anger and unjust feelings and bitter words are forming is more senseless and dastardly than flaunting a mistress before your wife while you are trying to tell her you love her.

——: A rather unfortunate figure of speech, but you make your point!

Leader: I know I've used an ugly figure — but it expresses an even uglier situation. And come to think of it, isn't it horribly ugly of us to say we believe in God, and reverence him, when we persist in making a travesty of our professed religion?

——: " To err is human." We are but imperfect humans.

——: Yes, imperfect. But to be forgiven is divine.

Leader: Right. Both of you. And the wonder of it is that both human and divine forgiveness always seem ours merely for the asking.

——: All we have to do is to ask for forgiveness.

——: After *first* being penitent.

The group have been together nearly two hours, but a mother who has said little asks: " Before we leave tonight, I hope somebody will help me to find out how old a child is supposed to be before parents begin praying with him. I understand the main idea that most of you have: that we are to pray *with* children, not just *hear* them say words. And I suppose that means no memorizing of little verses."

——: I don't think we need to say that ready-made prayers, of the right sort, are out entirely. My idea is that through absorption, through hearing verse prayers — such as those Mary Alice Jones has collected in her little book *First Prayers for Little Children* — a child will *want* to join in and learn, almost before he knows it. That was our experience with Kathy; she liked to say these prayers almost as soon as she learned to talk. We never insisted that she try to memorize them. But of course she did. Then she and I started, when she was about three and a half or four years old, to branch out. She was making up jingles anyway, experimenting with words, and that seemed to mean that she was ready to use her own language and original ideas in praying.

——: That's good. In our family we did that too. But I often wondered, when Charles was thanking God for every one of us — every last cousin and aunt, the cat and the milk pitcher and all the rest — if we hadn't rushed religion on him. It makes sense to wait until children are older — say about seven or eight — and can have greater capacity for appreciation and thankfulness before we verbalize sacred things too much.

——: That does make sense, but I've always been afraid that if that idea were followed too literally our own children would not get the habit of prayer.

——: Who wants prayer to be a habit — like brushing teeth? Not I.

——: I don't mean " habit "; not exactly, I guess. But after all, isn't there something in forming habits?

——: There's something in it all right, but the main idea is to develop the *attitude* for prayer.

——: I see. Then if my little boys *feel* thankful, and feel loving, you mean that they will *want* to pray; and that they will somehow get the idea that God is the source of all that's good.

——: Yes, that's about it. And they can also learn that they *need* to ask God to help them to be good — to share their toys and to help their mother with simple chores — just learn to grow up being considerate and helpful, instead of selfish and expecting to have the world wait on them all the time.

Leader: Would you say that the child's disposition to pray arises in much the same way in which he learns good manners? Good manners don't come as the result of our drilling children in manners. They come as the child lives with courteous, considerate parents.

——: Horrors! Here we are again, back to the poor parents — the source of all that's *bad* in child life!

——: *And* the source of all that's *good* too! Don't forget that.

Leader: Exactly. The awful truth is that, whether we want to acknowledge it or not, we are the only God a little child can know, at least until he is well along in the school years.

——: Pretty sobering stuff we're talking about now. I begin to see what the people mean who say that if the adults closest to the little child can't demonstrate something of God's nature, it's futile for them to *talk* God, and prayer, and how Jesus loves everybody.

——: First the child *experiences* the love of parents; he *sees* that they love each other, that this mysterious God to whom they pray in thanksgiving and in petition must be helping them to be better people; *then* he wants to do the same, and to *be* like his parents. Is that right? (Nods of agreement.)

——: Then the child is ready to put his prayer mood, his trusting mood, into the words of prayer. For he trusts his parents, loves them, and therefore is able to love and trust in God. So, he can talk *to* God, and talk *about* God. But not before. Good, thank you. I have the idea now. All this reminds me of the book by Manwell and Fahs *Consider the Children — How They Grow*. I'm going to read that book again.

These group conversations may serve to indicate how, when informal, friendly talk is neither a mere gab fest nor a rigidly structured discussion, persons are being educated. New ideas are born, and old ideas are examined so that they begin to take on vitality precisely because they become meaningful. Nor is the effective group conversation educational only on an intellectual level; it is also a means for re-educating personal feelings. Or, to state the proposition somewhat differently, the whole person is being helped to grow: at the ideational, emotional, and spiritual levels.

This sort of nurturing process touches people at the vital areas of their thinking and living. It is not so much a problem-solving process as it is a corporate experience in thinking and gaining insight. People come together partly because they have common concerns, and they remain because they learn to rely on the group. They trust and value each other's integrity as group fellowship enables them to share life in its most essential and significant dimensions. This corporate experience is quite the opposite of life in isolation, life outside the realm of social and emotional security. Rather, human and divine intercourse are experienced, through which not only communication but also *communion* is taking place. In communion, person with person, persons with the Spirit of truth — the Spirit of God — there is spiritual security.

8

CONCLUSION

❧　❧

ABOUT THE TIME the writing of these pages was drawing to an end, in the Midwestern city where I had gone for summer teaching, I had occasion to take my car to a garage to which I had never been before. To the men there I was an utter stranger. Now this car, being old, far from home, and much handled by mechanics, might well have received careless treatment. But presently it was responding, almost with animation, to the ministrations of a man whose genuine pleasure it was to serve me. Young and vigorous, he whistled at his work, pausing courteously to answer my numerous questions about the internal parts, with which he seemed joyfully at home. As for the shop foreman, his consideration excelled even that of his mechanic. Both men inspired confidence and made me feel that here, in fact, was a shop whose main motive was not one of raiding the customer's pocketbook. Two hours later, the bill presented me was reasonable; and presently the car was running flawlessly back to the campus.

Likewise, in the tiny restaurant where I was having early morning breakfasts before an eight o'clock class, I was being thanked, daily, for my patronage. Some mornings it would be the counterman-cook; others, the young waitress, who took my money and said thank you with polite sincerity. Their manner always struck me as that of a host and hostess instead of people mainly commercial. The pleasure of being with them for a few minutes at the beginning of the day was no less keen than that derived from the fatherly greetings of their aged Negro dishwasher, who seldom failed to emerge from behind the scenes at least once during breakfast in order to give his hearty friendliness to me as well as to the students who drifted over from the campus. Had the food been poor, instead of excellent, one would have still wanted the daily blessing of this place.

I

For some time I have resolved to venture where I may, on the lookout for evidence of man's fundamental kindliness and consideration toward the stranger in his midst. One may say that I but find that for which I look, but the fact remains that I have been finding a powerful amount of evidence that humankind is not so desperately accursed as it is represented to be by certain one-sided philosophical and theological views. To be sure, anecdotal experiences that reveal courtesy and thoughtfulness may appear as mere midgets beside the giants of national corruption and international despicableness. But let us not be mistaken by thinking that the midgets are weak because they are midgets. Right now, when personal, community, national, and world affairs are quick-paced and dangerous, and human existence tenuous, people do stop to reveal — without deliberation or self-interest — that it is their nature to serve their fellows unselfishly.

Nevertheless we have to reckon with ghastly evils, pervasive emotional illness, and sin. Though these are but a part and not the whole of man's nature, they throw him into a dilemma, and they demand astute consideration, both of thoughtful observers and of those who aspire to help their fellows to resolve debilitating tensions and defeat the devils that plague them. Especially does the victim of fear and despair, of enervating anxiety and blighting hopelessness, need help. So, also, the person whose zest for living has waned — whose life seems reduced from high purpose and meaning to arid endurance and futile effort — he too needs psychological and spiritual help. One's need for insight and restoration, together with the ways by which these are to be achieved, comprises the idea behind this volume.

This book is written, therefore, for people who want to find a deeper and more satisfying meaning in life. Because I am convinced that proper group relations yield otherwise unattainable emotional stability for the individual, I have devoted considerable attention to certain educational experiences through which the enrichment of fellowship is available to persons: in the community, neighborhood, family, the church, and in intimate associations with groups of friends. And because it is becoming increasingly recognized that both individual adults and children frequently need the particularly personal help to be found through counseling, selected reports have been offered from the counseling room.

But we simply cannot leave our needs at the doors of the professional workers of whatever kind. Sometimes it appears that the greatest single evil in modern society is the disposition to leave all the tasks of human betterment up to the specialists. Perhaps this tendency stems in the main from our kind of economy. As with the purchase of gadgets, so we assume that all that is required for possessing sound knowledge, sturdy bodies, healthy emotions, and strong characters is to have money in our pocket with which to make these values our own. This is as defeating as employing someone else to do our thinking, as silly as the notion of the man who would ask another to marry a wife for him.

One would think that life lived from crisis to crisis might goad us to intelligent inquiry about what understanding and action are essential for re-educating ourselves for the task of handling the vastly changed situations that have arisen in our world. Yet economic catastrophe, the debacle of war, and the decay of personal morality throughout society appear to have taught us very little. About the most that we do is to react in shock when an immediate danger storms upon us. So it is that in wartime men mouth slogans and cry that it is time " to get back to God." The trouble is that these returns usually are but temporary. Religious transients are the victims of the delusion that Church and religion are to be equated. In the hunger of his heart modern man naturally turns to the Church. And if he does, often as quickly he turns away again; for too seldom he finds there the spiritual quality of genuine fellowship that unconsciously he seeks. What he does become conscious of is that, instead of finding a needed spiritual quality, he is confronted by organized religion. The two are not, alas, the same.

Lamentable condition. Modern man — panicked by threat of war, bereft of stable family life, caught in an apartment rather than rooted in a community of neighborliness, committed to synthetic fraternity in luncheon club and lodge — is an isolate, a wanderer in a dry and thirsty land where people know machines instead of domestic animals, know Big Names of newspaper and television instead of the people in the adjoining flat, where lonely ones shuffle amid steel and concrete structures that have buried from sight the fields and woods of a pristine era forever dead.

It would prove instructive to churchmen were they to consider Ezekiel's visit to the valley of dry bones. What modern man wonders is, is the breath of life to return to the dry bones of the churches strewn across the land? Surely the Church will live again when men are drawn together in communion, person with person; when fellowship becomes flesh to replace organizational machinery and dull routine that have tried to pass as the living body. Ezekiel heard the Almighty address the bones:

" Behold, I will cause breath to enter into you. . . . I will lay sinews upon you, and will bring up flesh upon you, and cover you with skin . . . and ye shall live."

The clue to a vitalized spiritual community — a reborn Church — lies in the idea of making of the Church an intimate, face-to-face relationship in which one may experience the dynamic meaning of the worth of his fellows. For in fellowship there is power requisite for nurturing the individual, causing him to grow and to become strong enough to overcome the evils imbedded in him, as he releases the good native to him.

II

The key to a spiritual infusion of life where people live it — in community, neighborhood, family, business, school, and church — is the pastor. But the key is designed merely to unlock the door; what people do after they enter the household of faith is up to them. Mothers are of greater importance in the consistent guidance of the spiritual development of their children than a whole array of bishops and church teachers. Fathers whose character catches reflections of the spirit of the Man of Nazareth are more essential for the inculcation of righteousness and truth and integrity than all the figures in the Old and New Testaments combined. If this be true, then the inescapable responsibility for growing spiritually mature persons, and for building a secure world, rests with lay men and women. What can they do about it?

They can explore the rewarding possibilities to be found in community fellowship. A good portion of our communities have adult education groups which, though generally planned around textbooks, hobbies, and current affairs forums, can be extended to provide means for releasing individuals from the prison of social bias and emotional maladjustment. Ronald Lippitt in his book *Training in Community Relations* offers a record of what the exponents of group dynamics find possible when people desire to deal effectively with the problems of intergroup relations. *Resolving Social Conflicts*, by the late Kurt Lewin, a pioneer in group dynamics, presents a point of view and suggests a strategy to be used by social psychologists, educators, and others as they seek to influence community relations in a wholesome direction.

Every person of good will ought to get a new perspective of himself, so as to perceive that his life inevitably counts as a factor in making his community what it is. He may speak of human value as being inestimably greater than the material world about him; but at the same time he is likely to forget that he, his wife, his child, and his neighbor constitute that inestimable human value. True perspective should serve to make this citizen fully aware that if he but chooses to put at the center of his concerns the community and its individuals, he will find himself gathering like-minded people about him for the purpose of developing fellowship groups. He will find too that his community contains unsuspected resources for a corporate undertaking aimed at expressing good will among men. He will have his disappointments, of course; but he will encounter abundant reasons for gratification over the fact that people will respond in fellowship when they are guided by persons whose motives prove to be above reproach. The way for the conscientious citizen to begin is to look around and locate some need for neighborly expression.

The person bent on fostering community fellowship should work with existing agencies. In most instances, he does not have to start a new organization. There are exceptions, notably the National Citizens Commission for the Public Schools, but still the man of good will who is alerted for finding ways to serve his community, will ally himself with the parent-teacher association, the church, and other groups, and with them propagate two ideas: (1) adults can be challenged to grow through informal education groups which use such impressive mediums as role-playing and group discussion; and (2) groups of neighbors owe it to each other to share and celebrate their experiences in acts of service.

If we would find our lives, we must lose them in community and neighborhood service. But along with our individual service should go group thinking and planning, so as to prevent deterioration of motive and to make us intelligently responsible in whatever we may undertake. For instance, if we inform some community group that we have decided to move our family into the midst of people who represent many racial and national differences, we run the risk of giving the impression that we are engaged either in superficial experimentation or in patronizing the unfortunates of the community. We certainly want to avoid all appearance of a slumming expedition.

Laymen who undertake to purge their community of the vices of racially restrictive housing, neglected public education, corrupt town government, will link their efforts with honest lawyers, ethical parsons, democratic educators, and others who are independent and courageous enough to speak out. Groups of citizens whose actions carry forward the principles and ethical demands of the Judaeo-Christian tradition, will keep in mind that they are needed within the active membership of the churches. Before they go very far in their work toward educating the community and themselves, they will discover with startling clarity that their efforts require the sanction of organized religion and its Scriptural strength.

There will be times when community reformers will run into timid churchmen from whom no spiritual vigor is forthcoming. But these laymen should not turn away in disgust from the church; rather, they should attach themselves to it, cognizant of the fact that the power of religion is not really limited by its insensitive and ignorant priests. Then too there will come a day when a new leader of a particular church is to be chosen. That will be occasion for a listing of prophetic qualifications of the new parson to include the power of justice and mercy, fearlessly espoused. In this way groups of citizens who begin to serve their community as independents, so far as the church is concerned, will end up by empowering organized religion by their ethical and spiritual forces. Like family and church, community and church need each other. Perhaps of late too much has been said, in religious circles, about the need for the church to go to the community; more needs to be said about the community going to the church. Groups of citizens who purpose to establish fellowship within their community, will — if they advance far toward their goal — find themselves in the vanguard of those who go to the church, and, having gone, identify themselves with it. Then will fellowship abound, while community and persons move toward spiritual security.

III

As I conceive it, the neighborhood group can mean the difference between a place from which people escape at every opportunity, and a face-to-face gathering of persons who respect and care for each other; so much so that for them a chief joy of life lies in being together. In such a setting children as well as adults flourish amid warm and kindly affections. This is the quality that guarantees mental health and lays the groundwork for spiritual maturity.

It is not correct to say that today there is no substitute for the values of a more primitive era when neighbors united to conquer wilderness danger and frontier loneliness. We have other wildernesses now, and who will deny that urban society is lonely to its depths?

In Chapter 2 the neighbors faced the wilderness of prejudice when their attitude threatened to keep a would-be neighbor lonely. But because they knew how to think together instead of fighting each other's ideas, these people rose to the occasion and kept neighborliness alive.

Most of us encounter racial exclusiveness and similar threats in our own neighborhoods. Often we wonder if we as individuals can accomplish anything by way of expressing democracy and ethical religion. This wonder soon slips into doubt, and we hope we may be excused for not taking a courageous stand. We do not wish to be unpleasant to our kind, and so we drift into the popular frame of mind that keeps neighborhoods exclusively Gentile and white.

Were we to draw all the strength available from our neighborhoods as they now exist — be they as Gentile and as white as they may — we would enter into groups of persons who, together, could experience the real meaning of fellowship. This might well lead to the group's intention to expand democracy and ethics so as to draw into their fold the hitherto neglected and despised members of other races and religions.

People who live in a common geographic setting need to constitute themselves into a neighborhood group both for their own sake and for the sake of their community. When neighbors group themselves informally for the purpose of helping a family with a sick member, or pool their thinking as to what course to follow for solving some neighborhood problem, they have taken an initial step toward further group experience. When that is the case, people who live near each other's houses have begun to live close to each other. This, they have long sensed, is an answer to one of their most fundamental needs.

Anyone who would be a good neighbor should give thought to the matter. If you grew up among people who were neighborly, and came from a home where love predominated, you are already fitted to be a neighbor. But if all your life you have suffered from isolation and lack of affection, you are likely to be timid and socially withdrawn. Therefore, you will have to work much harder than some do at the problem of being neighborly. One step might take you next door to render help; for example, raking leaves. Let us suppose that your yard is clean, you know your neighbor is on a business trip and his wife has her hands full taking care of young children. Surely, now, you can go next door and begin raking.

If, in addition to the above circumstances, your neighbor's wife is ill, then you and your wife can take turns in seeing that she is cared for, her children fed and taken into your home during a part of the day. Within a few days other neighbors will probably follow your example and join you. By the time matters are righted you and the neighbors will have learned to like each other, mainly because you have spent some time together doing something that needed to be done. In the process, you may find it easier to greet people. And the chances are you will find yourself loosed inside from the halter that through the years has held you in check when you felt inclined to go out of your way on behalf of someone besides yourself and your family.

Presently you may notice that people are beginning to have parties and other gatherings in the neighborhood. You join them and are warmly greeted because people know that although you have never had much to say in the neighborhood, you are the one who first gave help to the family next door. The neighbors take to dealing with issues that concern them and their children. Slowly you are drawn into the discussions. You find that your opinions hold up fairly well, but you begin to wish that you could lead the conversation, or direct a discussion, as skillfully as the postman or the repairman who lives down the street. Carefully you watch the best leader, studying his methods. You note that above all else he is a friendly person, and is fair to every point of view. One night you ask him how he came to be so gifted in handling so many different topics. He tells you what he reads and that he goes to an evening class each week held at the local college. You learn that this man has worked to perfect his ability as a discussant and as a leader. Now you know what to do, and you do it. You study.

You will find that even professional people often fail as leaders in a discussion. More than that, they fail as participants in a discussion, for they may try to dominate the conversation, resort to debate, or divert the group's attention from the issues at hand. The result of all this is that democracy is weakened, group life sours, committees in education, business, government, and other affairs prove inept. What can correct the deficiency of discussion leaders? They will have to be trained for this role at least as diligently as public speakers are trained. Especially teachers and preachers ought to have thorough training in guiding group thinking, for a major part of their professional life is not spent in lecturing and in preaching, but in chairmaning committees, leading informal group discussion, presiding at sundry forums. And what is true about professional people holds true also about corporation presidents, business executives, legislators, and all who serve on committees.

The final word here is that almost any member of a democracy who aspires to be worthy of this privilege would do well to have training as a discussion leader. Furthermore he should study for effective participation as a group member. *Handbook of Group Discussion*, by Wagner and Arnold, can be used to good effect. By attending a university extension course or a community school's evening class, you will find opportunity to equip yourself in the art of leading groups and in taking part as a constructive group member. In the past, classes in public speaking have been popular for adults, but far more worth-while is the job of learning how to lead a group so that the best of common experiences may be strengthened and the most valid of corporate thinking may be enjoyed.

Good group relations seldom happen by accident. It takes a skilled leader (plus individual members' competency in handling ideas and human relations) to create a good group. The neighborhood group offers one of the best settings for leaders and discussants to improve their skill as members of this and of larger units of society. More than skill, they develop social rootage which lends itself to emotional and spiritual security.

IV

An able counselor of long experience has said that he spends a major part of his time with young people whose fathers are professional men. Teachers, professors, parsons, physicians, psychiatrists, social workers, and more — many of whom know the theory of proper child nurture — not infrequently fail as parents. People sometimes point to them not so much in ridicule as by way of discounting their fancy educational and psychological theories. But it is not their theories and knowledge about child care and family relations that are incorrect; what is wrong is that professional men too seldom get around to investing enough time with their families so as to make sound knowledge function.

The first step toward changing this all too prevalent situation calls upon professional people to take stock of their practices.

The social worker will conclude that he must limit his helping of families, and increase his own family's unity.

The physician may decide to deliver fewer babies in order to deliver his wife and children from their sense of loss of him.

The psychiatrist will begin to conserve enough energy to talk things over within his own family.

The teacher can begin to express through his home the democracy he articulates in the classroom.

The professor will read and write fewer books and work and play more with his family.

And the minister will learn that his service to the family of God is better when he first serves his wife and children.

Family life is more easily talked and written about than lived. When children buzz around us continuously, mental and physical fatigue causes us to respond irritatedly. Instead of stopping to play, as a child's annoying interruption is designed to get us to do, we mutter, ignore him, or punish him. We have to be " fair to the bees," with the same sense of elementary justice evidenced by a first-grader. This child was half lost from sight in a field of daisies. When his mother called to him, the child found his way out blocked by bees. A man working nearby with a mowing machine advised him to wait until the daisies were cut, and the bees thus removed. " But that would not be fair to the bees," the child responded.

Here are four simple observations for the professional man's thought as he resolves to be fair to the bees: (1) Investment of time with the family yields dividends of happiness, group solidarity, fun, and growth toward maturity that can never otherwise be attained. (2) If time seems unavailable, it is likely true that a proper sense of values is the real shortage. (3) When a family has turned into a matriarchy, probably the reason is not so much the desire of the wife as the abdication of the father. (4) Family fellowship, created by respect, permissiveness, love, and sacrifice, is the best single guarantee of wholesome group relations and of spiritual security for the individual.

But it is not only the busy professional man's family that today suffers because parents do not give themselves unreservedly to their children and to each other. Early America, when most families were farm families, saw parents and children working together on the land and about the house, going to church together, and having picnics and parties with neighboring families. Now industrial America splits the family in as many directions as its individual members. The father leaves home for most of the day. Each child goes off to a different classroom, if not to a different school from that attended by his brothers and sisters. Mother hurries through her household chores alone, and, if she is not gainfully employed, goes to the grocery store or to the home of a neighbor unknown to the rest of her family. For recreation, children scatter to city play lots, one parent goes to a lodge, the other to a club.

As a result of this dispersion of the family, both children and adults sense a vague loss, or find themselves caught in surly feelings that increase their neglect by other members of the family. From neglect there invariably flows apathy or resentment and hostility. If these feelings are to be counteracted within the home, parents will have to start seeing to it that each member of the family, of whatever age, gets his due attention. And this attention means that his needs, his wants, his interests, are fully attended to in a very individual manner.

When parents follow this course of action, they will learn that a child is not receiving suitable attention when a mother cooks with one hand and fastens his jacket with the other, or when a father divides his glance between Junior's new drawing and the newspaper. It is our undivided attention that a child most desires and certainly deserves.

" But if I give my daughter my full attention," it is often said, " instead of her stopping silly pranks to get my attention, she demands more and more from me." The answer to that is that this mother probably has a lot of catching up to do in the business of showing her child adequate attention before the child is convinced that her mother really cares.

But if children need parents' undivided attention in frequent and ample doses, so also does each parent need from the other full interest and attention. Neither family unity nor married love happen by some fortunate set of circumstances. Both have to be cultivated by regularity in sharing responsibility, exchanging ideas, planning together for use of money, building reserves for protection in sickness and old age, taking vacations, rendering service to others, and reverencing God.

The above is not addressed only to white-collar families who nowadays are expected to read books, participate in study groups, and take a reasonable approach to creating lasting fellowship and security within the home, but also to the workingman. He it is who often has shorter working hours, more money, and therefore greater opportunity for following these suggestions than many of his white-collar or professional friends. In all frankness it should be said that the " workingman " ought now to begin working diligently at the job of guiding his family into new ways of conducting their relations. In this he can get help from reading good magazines and books. Let him master the ideas found in the monthly *Parents' Magazine*. He would do well to include his family in this publication's list of a million and a quarter circulation. Let him also subscribe to *The Christian Home,* the best and largest monthly magazine in its field. Catherine Mackenzie's *Parent and Child,* and *How to Help Your Child in School,* by Mary and Lawrence Frank, can be read with profit by any parent who can read a newspaper. *Sex Fulfillment in Marriage,* by the Groveses would strengthen most readers' homes. Other books referred to in this volume will interest the general reader who wants to bring the resources of education, psychology, and religion to the experience of enriching family living.

In this book, and in my earlier volume *The Modern Parent and the Teaching Church,* I have tried to make sufficiently clear the impressive fact that the family needs the church " as a fountain needs a reservoir." In Chapter 6 I have enumerated specific steps to be taken by family and church as they co-ordinate their nurture for developing spiritually mature persons. Co-ordinated nurture carried forward by family and church requires a program quite different from the usual church school program, or any weekday plan for teaching religion. Before home and church nurture can succeed, parents will have to be led by the church through a process of adult spiritual growth that can overflow into all the experiences of the family in home and community.

There are at least two essentials involved: (1) parents committed to the undertaking; and (2) churches ready and competent to conduct radically different parent education.

V

A ten-year-old boy sat with me in the church conference room. " People have troubles, many, many troubles. Cancer, polio, tuberculosis, getting killed in war, not enough money — all kinds of troubles. Everybody has troubles."

" *Everybody?* "

" Yes; and *I* have plenty. Can't sleep at night; wake up afraid those big red things are about to get me."

This boy had been to see me several times before. From him and others I had learned the essential facts of his life. His father had been a gambler — a " bookie " — but had given it up for a trucker's job. About the time the smaller pay check began coming in, the mother deserted the family. The boy soon developed a tic and fell prey to numbers of fears. Though gifted with superior intelligence and privileged to enjoy steady schooling, recreation clubs, summer camping, and religious education, he remained emotionally insecure. The educational and recreational institutions of society could not reach him at the point of his deep need, and neither was organized religion helping him to become spiritually mature.

Relief came from an accumulation of simple steps. Within the privacy of the conference room the boy could talk at will, unburdening himself of countless irrational fears (clarification of his perplexities contributed largely to the progress made), and recounting the long history of his parents' deceptions. Most pronounced in this record was the way his parents took him — as a child of three — to the hospital. Already, before that experience, the child had learned to fear hospitals and doctors. He was told that he was going to a big building where some nice men would give him presents. What he found were robed men, no presents, a big cloth forced over his head, ether, and pain. It all added up to fright and distrust. Both reactions stayed with the child through the years until he found therapy in the counseling room.

There is promise in the growing program for training ministers, directors of religious education, schoolteachers, and other nonmedical workers to listen to children and help them to gain freedom from their fears. For pastors and directors of religious education the new journal *Pastoral Psychology* is instructive. *So You Want to Help People,* by Rudolph M. Wittenberg, is a mental hygiene primer for group leaders who want to assist individuals by first understanding them in group relations.

Ruth Cunningham and associates have a book, *Understanding Group Behavior of Boys and Girls,* mainly suitable for schoolteachers and studious parents, but club and church leaders ought also to study this work as a means for improving their guidance of growing persons toward maturity. Simpler printed helps may be gotten from the Child Study Association (132 E. 74th Street, New York 21) and from the Bureau of Publications, Teachers College, Columbia University.

Scores of church councils and individual churches have recently been holding institutes on family life and religion's place in fostering spiritual growth. Study groups inside and out of the churches abound with topics for reading and discussion related to nurturing children and encouraging the home to meet its responsibility for child guidance. All these are seeds of promise.

And so the planting goes on. Nor is this the whole story;

the total effort would take hundreds of pages for its telling.

Consider briefly the watering and cultivating of the seed. Here are seven directives:

1. Mothers and fathers of the young child will join with a group of other parents and study child care, as psychologists conceive it. These groups are best when they spring up more or less spontaneously, and when they are, at least at times, guided by the strong church that can combine educational, psychological, and spiritual insights.

2. Community nursery schools, in many instances sponsored by the churches, should become a goal for every American community. Fathers no less than mothers will participate in the life of these schools.

3. Laymen ought to consider establishing a National Laymen's Committee on Religious Nurture, somewhat along the lines of the National Citizens Commission for the Public Schools. Spiritual nurture by organized religion ought not to be expected to thrive so long as people assume that religious education is to be left to pastors and religious educators.

4. Laymen and ministers will, eventually by necessity, seriously undertake a community approach to strengthening organized religion. Groups of neighbors who are now concerned to abolish racial discrimination, sectarian exclusiveness, and other stumbling blocks in spiritual nurture need not wait for the distant day when religion is to be reorganized along community lines. They can begin now, in their neighborhood groups, to work toward this objective.

5. Parents, teachers, leaders of boys' and girls' clubs, anyone who guides the growth of children will take what steps may be necessary toward securing any needed personal therapy. Spiritual security on the part of the young, being dependent on religiously mature adult personalities, can be assured only when adults are right within themselves, and truly right with God.

6. Parents and teachers will be alert to refer children and youth to child guidance clinics, and to the increasing number of churches that have ministers and educators ready to help individuals to develop spiritual security. For children do have problems which, if not solved before the adult years, will issue in insecure

lives incapable of giving and receiving love. During youth and later, the final rooting out of emotional difficulty requires a spiritual process no less than psychological therapy.

7. In each of these points the lay reader will perceive that he is the leader who — like the educator, the psychologist, and the minister — is to give his energies to a nurturing process that can reach people at their personal depths and release their native capacities to grow into social, emotional, and spiritual maturity. Therefore, every lay leader will foster community fellowship as a corporate expression of his personal battle against social isolation and individual loneliness and fear. He will learn to commune with his fellows in family, neighborhood, and church, for in these areas the genius of human and divine intercourse reaches fruition in spiritually mature men and women.

Date Due			BROADMAN B P SUPPLIES